THE STRUGGLE FOR STABILITY IN
EARLY MODERN EUROPE

THE STRUGGLE
FOR STABILITY IN
EARLY MODERN
EUROPE

THEODORE K. RABB

Princeton University

New York
OXFORD UNIVERSITY PRESS
1975

Copyright © 1975 by Oxford University Press, Inc.
Library of Congress Catalogue Card Number: 75-4207
ISBN-13: 978-0-19-501956-8
ISBN 0-19-501956-3 (pbk.)

23 25 27 29 28 26 24 22

Printed in the United States of America
on acid-free paper

For Susannah, Jonathan, and Jeremy

PREFACE

This essay was written in response to an apparently growing need. During the last half-dozen years, my classes in Early Modern History have made me increasingly aware that the "general crisis of the seventeenth century" thesis, about which so much has been written, and whose importance as a problem in current research seems solidly established, frequently confuses rather than enlightens. Even advanced students come away from a reading of the articles published in *Past & Present* and the related literature with the impression that chaos reigns, that there is no way of reaching firm conclusions or imposing a coherent framework on so contentious a subject. Nor have the scholars who have produced these works offered much solace. Although many resort to the term "crisis," and it has become a standby in introductory textbooks, hardly any two treatments agree in the meaning of the word, let alone its implications for an understanding of the sixteenth and seventeenth centuries. For students above all, but also for specialists, it may well be time to call a halt: to examine what has been accomplished, and to see if a comprehensive assessment is now possible.

What follows is an elaboration, and more detailed statement, of an interpretation—in part a reordering of familiar materials, in part an attempt to find new connections—that has seemed to be of some benefit to uncertain students and of some utility to a number of colleagues in the field. There is the additional justification for offering it to a wider audience that the two centuries very roughly between Reformation and Enlightenment have traditionally been the most shapeless in European history. Indeed, as we will see, it was precisely because of the fragmented scholarship produced before World War II that the "crisis" thesis could have such an impact. Unfortunately, the divisions and perplexities it aroused quickly dissolved its role as the creator of a new means of organizing the period. Thus a new overview, building on that first effort, may be appropriate, and my hope is that this book, though too short to accomplish more than a sketch of a new framework, will at least prod current scholarly interests toward an acceptable synthesis, whether in opposition to, or by an extension of, the arguments that are put forward here.

To establish the context, the first few sections review the historiography of the subject. I then suggest, in sections V-X, a new chronological and analytic framework for the period. Finally, the last two sections offer some possible reasons for the great change on which the interpretation focuses, and a brief look to the future.

If such rapid traversal of an immense area seems foolhardy, to put it mildly, I can only respond by quoting the justification so aptly volunteered by Joseph Meeker under similar circumstances, in *The Comedy of Survival:*

> A hopeless attempt to see things whole is at least as worthy as the equally hopeless task of isolating fragments for intensive study.

He continues, "and much more interesting," but I am willing to let the case rest without flinging down that additional gauntlet.

* * *

Many colleagues and students have commented on this essay, and the modifications they have suggested have transformed it, in the course of four years and numerous revisions, beyond recognition. All responsibility is, naturally, mine alone, but I must record my gratitude to those—especially those who disagreed with my views—who forced me to hammer out an argument which may now have some use for others who study or teach the period. If I cannot record all the readers, I must convey my appreciation to those who particularly encouraged or recognizably influenced the pages that follow: Renato Barahona, Philip Benedict, Theodore Brown, John Elliott, Christopher Friedrichs, Charles George, James Henretta, Michael Heyd, Josef Konvitz, Irving Lavin, Orest Ranum, John Schuster, Lawrence Stone, and Charles Tilly.

To the prime encourager, my wife, no expression of appreciation could be adequate.

Princeton   T.K.R.
November 1974

CONTENTS

❀

ILLUSTRATIONS

❁

"The road to resolution lies by doubt:
The next way home's the farthest way about."

—Francis Quarles, *Emblems* (1635),
Book IV, No. 2, Epigram 2.

THE STRUGGLE FOR STABILITY IN
EARLY MODERN EUROPE

I

THE PROBLEM

Momus (pointing to Mars): Thy Wars brought nothing about.

. . .

Janus: 'Tis well an Old Age is out,
Chronos: And time to begin a New.

—John Dryden, *The Secular Masque* from
The Pilgrim, lines 88-91.

A historian must take pause when in three short lines a poet distills the argument of many, many pages. Yet Dryden's oft-quoted observation, put in the mouths of iconographically well-chosen Greek and Roman gods, does describe in a few words a development which this essay will attempt at some length to describe and explain. My only disagreement with Dryden is that I believe the wars did bring something about. But the sense that an age is passing, which is so strong not only in his writing but throughout the culture of his times, is central to the understanding of the late seventeenth century that I wish to propose. What I will be trying to demonstrate is that Europe entered a new era very roughly during the middle third of the century, and that the best indication of this profound transformation is the very different atmosphere that reigned in the succeeding decades. Between, say, the early 1630's and the early 1670's (though it would be foolish to insist on crisp cut-off points in so far-reaching a process) there was a change in direction more dramatic and decisive than any that occurred in a

forty-year period between the beginnings of the Reformation and
the French Revolution. And it is precisely by recognizing how different Europe's situation was in the *aftermath* of these events than it
had been during, or immediately preceding, the great shift that we
can come to appreciate the extent of the alteration that had been
wrought. As in modern physics, the existence of the phenomenon
itself can become more perceptible when one focuses on its consequences.

A quick, impressionistic index, both of the new sensibility and of
the new social and political relationships, is revealed by a number
of obvious contrasts: between the taste of Rubens and the taste of
Claude; between the commitments of Milton and the commitments
of Dryden; between the aspirations of Charles I and those of his
son, Charles II; between the ambitions of Condé in the 1640's (not
unlike those held by his father or great-grandfather in the 1610's
and 1560's) and then during the last few years before his death in
1686; between the career of Wallenstein and the career of Eugène;
between the reception of Galileo and the reception of Newton; between the angst-ridden striving for order of a Descartes or a
Hobbes and the confidence of a Locke; between the image of Gustavus Adolphus, "the champion of Protestantism," and Charles XII,
the defender of Sweden's "great-power position"; between the policies of Paul V and Innocent XI; between a society vulnerable and
then relatively impervious to witchcraft panics. In all these cases
the years around 1700 appear more ordered, more assured about accepted conventions, less divided, less prone to vast and uncontrolled
strivings in new directions, and less passionate about commitments—
in sum, more settled and relaxed—than the preceding years. The
comparison is relative, of course, not absolute. Disorder, division,
and commitment were by no means absent from the 1690's; but
their menace was less than it had been in the 1630's or 1640's, and,
most important, they were *considered* less menacing by contemporaries. The chief subject of this essay is thus a change in perception: its nature, causes, and consequences.

By stressing the difference of the latter part of the seventeenth
century I shall be drawing on the findings of a number of scholars.
Perhaps the first to see this period as a time of fundamental change

was Paul Hazard, whose classic *La Crise de la conscience euro-péenne* was published nearly half a century ago.[1] Since then, many historians have purported to see a "crisis" taking place somewhat earlier than Hazard's opening date of 1680, and on the whole their chronology seems more appropriate to my schema.[2] But they, on the other hand, have given almost no attention to the period with which Hazard was in fact dealing, and which this essay will be stressing. Indeed, the emphases of the present work are such that it might well be characterized as a "post-crisis" interpretation—a designation that has a double justification, both chronological and historiographical. It denotes, first, the view that the changed circumstances of the *end* of the seventeenth century, that is, in the "post-crisis" era, provide the best evidence for the belief that a genuine and significant transformation had taken place at mid-century. Second, it indicates an attempt to go beyond the literature on the "crisis," to provide a new perspective on the themes that historians have studied so extensively during the past twenty years, since Eric Hobsbawm first wrote of a "general crisis."[3] In other words, by highlighting the later period this essay also seeks to re-formulate and reshape a scholarly controversy: to confront a "struggle for stability" both in Early Modern Europe and among its recent students.

Before any such enterprise can be undertaken, however, we must first examine (as we will in sections II and III) the background out of which the reassessment arises. For the historiography of the century and a half extending approximately from the death of Calvin to the birth of Voltaire has been quite distinctive. From the generation of Ranke until after World War II, its main concerns were significantly different from those that dominated research into the preceding and succeeding periods, the Reformation and the Enlightenment. And in recent times it has enjoyed a ferment of reinterpretation unmatched by any field of European his-

---

1. (Paris, 1935). The translation, by J. L. May, was published as *The European Mind, 1680-1715* (Cleveland and New York, 1963).
2. See below, notes 21-24.
3. Eric Hobsbawm, "The Overall Crisis of the European Economy in the Seventeenth Century," *Past & Present*, No. 5 (1954), 33-53.

tory. My main emphasis, inevitably, will be on this burst of activity, on its results and its implications for the future, and above all on the question of whether there are now grounds for the creation of a new framework, a new shape, to guide studies of the sixteenth and seventeenth centuries.

II

SCHOLARLY FRAGMENTATION AND THE ORIGINS OF THE "CRISIS" THESIS

Fifty years ago the period seemed to have virtually no structure at all. Indeed, the most famous characterization of the seventeenth century during the 1920's was Alfred North Whitehead's "the century of genius," which is about as atomized a description of a hundred years as one can imagine.[4] Yet hardly anything more coherent or comprehensive was available to the interested student. Very few historians after Ranke had ventured to analyze general developments, and almost none had ventured into European-wide assessments. Whereas the Reformation and Enlightenment obviously could not be investigated solely within a narrow national compass, the century and a half in the middle seemed naturally fragmented. After all, one could find a "golden age" in just about every major country—Cervantes' Spain, Louis XIV's France, Elizabethan England, Rembrandt's Holland, Gustavus' Sweden, Christian IV's Denmark. Since this was such a heroic time, most historians were content to study their own country in isolation. When, by contrast, it was a time of disaster, as in central Europe during the Thirty Years' War, there were equally good reasons for limiting the coverage—in this case, so as to battle over the perennial question of the place of the war in German (or occasionally Czech) history, all the while ignoring its wider ramifications.[5]

4. A. N. Whitehead, *Science and the Modern World* (New York, 1925). Chapter III is entitled "Century of Genius," and the label has been adopted by, among others, the blurb writer for Stuart Hampshire, ed., *The Age of Reason: The 17th Century Philosophers* (New York, 1956).
5. A classic instance of this historiography is the literature on the *Wallensteinfrage*, which has focused repeatedly on the question of whether the

Even when broader themes did appear, such as absolutism, constitutionalism, or the Counter-Reformation, they seemed to have major relevance only to two or three states at a time. France and Brandenburg-Prussia were the exemplars of absolutism, England and Holland (in total isolation) of constitutionalism, and Spain, Italy, and central Europe of the Counter-Reformation. Repeatedly it was the local that was emphasized—in the great works of Gardiner, Firth, Scott, and their contemporaries, for example, Englishmen usually behave in a vacuum, and one wonders where poor Charles I got his strange ideas about monarchical power.[6] It is not surprising, therefore, that Whitehead, looking over the century, should have taken the ultimate reductionist approach, emphasizing individual genius as the chief unity in seventeenth-century European history.

The English-speaking world was particularly indifferent to developments outside England or America in this period. Until World War II major contributions to non-Anglo-Saxon studies had been made by only five men: Motley, Hamilton, Clark, Merriman, and Ogg.[7] And in the United States in the 1940's and 1950's only Mat-

---

generalissimo belongs most appropriately in German or Czech history, and then addresses itself to his qualities or deficiencies from the nationalist point of view. The most notable examples of the German/favorable and the Czech/hostile interpretations are, respectively, Heinrich Ritter von Srbik, *Wallensteins Ende: Ursachen, Verlauf und Folgen der Katastrophe* (Salzburg, 1952) and Josef Pekař, *Wallenstein 1630-1634, Tragödie einer Verschwörung*, I (Berlin, 1937). The Thirty Years' War is a subject not confined to one state, and therefore is all the more significant for having been treated consistently within various national frameworks.

6. S. R. Gardiner, *History of England from the Accession of James I. to the Outbreak of the Civil War 1603-1642* (London, 1883-84); Charles Firth, *Oliver Cromwell and the Rule of the Puritans in England* (Oxford, 1900); W. R. Scott, *The Constitution and Finance of English, Scottish, and Irish Joint-Stock Companies to 1720* (Cambridge, 1912). These three historians produced the most important works on Stuart history during the generation preceding World War I, and indeed their contribution was hardly equaled until after World War II. The equivalent scholars among their contemporaries on the Continent were equally parochial in their research.

7. J. L. Motley, *The Rise of the Dutch Republic. A History* (New York, 1856) and *History of the United Netherlands* (New York, 1861-68); E. J. Hamilton, *American Treasure and the Price Revolution in Spain, 1501-1650*

tingly and Wolf offered the training, research, and study from which a wider interest might grow.[8] The situation was, if anything, marginally worse in England.[9] And in the two principal centers of the historical profession on the Continent, Germany and France, the exceptions were only slightly more numerous. The *Propyläen Weltgeschichte* and *Peuples et Civilisations* series produced volumes between the two World Wars that did survey all of Europe and more, but such vast co-operative undertakings rarely achieve a compelling and unified view of a period, and these were no exception.[10] Their emphasis was heavily on political and diplomatic history, in which they perceived few universal themes. This was true, too, of the international researches of a handful of individual schol-

---

(Cambridge, Mass., 1934) and "American Treasure and the Rise of Capitalism, 1500-1700," *Economica*, IX (1929), 338-57; G. N. Clark, *The Seventeenth Century* (Oxford, 1929); R. B. Merriman, *The Rise of the Spanish Empire in the Old World and the New* (New York, 1918-34), *Six Contemporaneous Revolutions* (Oxford, 1938), and *Suleiman the Magnificent, 1520-1566* (Cambridge, Mass., 1944); and David Ogg, *Europe in the Seventeenth Century* (London, 1928) and *Louis XIV* (London, 1933). It is only fair to mention that a number of economic historians, notably C. H. Haring, S. L. Mims, and C. W. Cole, did write substantial works on Continental history, but they did not affect the over-all understanding of the history of the period, as did the historians mentioned above.

8. Mattingly taught at Columbia University, Wolf at the University of Minnesota. After Merriman's retirement from Harvard these two provided the only graduate training in early modern European history available at an American institution until the emergence of such Mattingly students as Herbert Rowen, Robert Kingdon, and De Lamar Jensen, and their contemporaries, like Andrew Lossky, in the 1950's.

9. Apart from Clark and Ogg, the chief sources on early modern Europe used by Oxford and Cambridge undergraduates until the 1950's were *The Cambridge Modern History* and J. M. Thompson's *Lectures on Foreign History 1494-1789* (Oxford, 1925; third edition, 1956). The only scholar of the 1930's who devoted most of his work to Continental affairs was Trevor Davies of Oxford. Significantly, Thompson was eventually superseded by V. H. H. Green's *Renaissance and Reformation* (London, 1952), written by a specialist in English history.

10. *Propyläen-Weltgeschichte*, Vols. 5 and 6 (Berlin, 1930 and 1931); *Peuples et Civilisations*, ed. Louis Halphen and Philippe Sagnac, Vols. VIII and IX: Henri Hauser and Augustin Renaudet, *Les Débuts de l'âge moderne* (Paris, 1929) and Henri Hauser, *La Prépondérance espagnole (1559-1660)* (Paris, 1933).

ars interested in a broader canvas, the best of whom was Georges Pagès.[11] The one truly ambitious attempt to embrace all of Europe in a self-avowed "unifying system," and to give the seventeenth century a distinct place in history, was the work of a Swede, Eli Heckscher. But the criticisms of his massive monograph came so fast and furious that interpretations remained as divided as before.[12]

It was after World War II that a dramatic change swept over the historiography, especially in France, England, and America. Some of the older traditions continued—for instance, in the publications of one of Pagès's more notable students, V.-L. Tapié, and in the continuing vitality of national historiography—but it was clear that an increasing number of scholars were engaged in areas outside their native language.[13] Although the changes in approach and subject matter were far more important, the numerical growth was not an insubstantial measure of the new vitality of the field. In 1966 it became possible to found a Society of Early Modern Historians, centered at Brigham Young University, and its April 1971 newsletter already described the research of close to 400 members in Europe and the United States, together with the dissertation subjects of over 200 of their doctoral students. The most spectacular progress has taken place in the United States, where a trickle of

11. The finest work on a general subject of seventeenth-century European history published between the World Wars was Pagès's *La Guerre de trente ans* (Paris, 1939). He had originally made his name with *Le Grand Electeur et Louis XIV, 1660-1688* (Paris, 1905).

12. First published in Swedish in 1931, Heckscher's two volumes appeared in English as *Mercantilism* (London, 1935) three years after a German edition. The best introduction to the controversy the book inspired is W. E. Minchinton, *Mercantilism: System or Expediency?* (Lexington, Mass., 1969). Heckscher entitled Part I of the work "Mercantilism as a Unifying System."

13. In addition to French history, Tapié's interests have been mainly diplomatic and central European history: *La Politique étrangère de la France et le début de la guerre de trente ans (1616-1621)* (Paris, 1934), *Les Relations entre la France et l'Europe centrale de 1661-1715* (Paris, 1958), and *Monarchie et peuples du Danube* (Paris, 1969); he has recently also worked on the history of art: see note 136, below. One has but to mention the major contributions of Michael Roberts to Swedish history, John Elliott to Spanish history, and Charles Boxer to Dutch and Portuguese history, to indicate the change in historiography in England alone.

those who studied anything but the Anglo-Saxons in the seventeenth century has turned into a flood. But the vitality can be seen in most Western countries—important contributions to current debates have come from, among other places, the Netherlands, Denmark, and Italy[14]—and, most significant of all, the research on the seventeenth century has had repercussions in many other areas. For it has been the content of the new work, not its volume, that has had the most pregnant consequences. A splintered specialty has attained in a few years a coherence, a sense of purpose, and a degree of excitement whose result has been to turn a bridesmaid into a bride. And the sources of this new glamor are not far to seek.

* * *

The first impetus came, quite simply, from the French, and in particular from one of the most fertile influences in recent historiography, the VIe Section of the École Pratique des Hautes Études in Paris. Their great journal, *Annales*, was founded in 1929 by a medievalist, Marc Bloch, and a Reformation scholar, Lucien Febvre. Their part in reshaping our notions of what social and cultural history ought to be has been enormous, and eventually the late sixteenth and the seventeenth century became the principal beneficiaries of the *Annales* school's attention. For when the journal resumed publication after the war, the men who gradually came to dominate the VIe Section were scholars with a prime interest in this period: Fernand Braudel, the Chaunus, Le Roy Ladurie, and Pierre Goubert. Braudel, in particular, virtually reopened the late sixteenth century as a subject of study with his enormous book on the Mediterranean world in the reign of Philip II, published in 1949.[15] In the same year the French founded a journal entitled *XVII Siècle*. Thereafter they enjoyed a growing international influence, particularly as a result of their concern with local, peasant society in pre-industrial times, analyzed through demographic data and attention to such forces as plague, subsistence crises, urban growth, and changes in family life.

This microcosmic and "material" history has had repercussions

14. See below, notes 29, 31, 37, and 40.
15. *La Méditerranée et le monde méditerranéen a l'époque de Philippe II* (Paris, 1949); an English translation of the second edition (1966) by Siân Reynolds was published in London in 1972 and 1973.

throughout the profession, but it has been particularly invigorating in early modern studies. Its impact is no doubt partly due to the sharp contrast it presents to previous work, both because of its concern with the masses rather than elites, and because in peasant life the regularities seem more encompassing than, for example, the Counter-Reformation or absolutism. Through social analysis the period takes on more of a "structure," to use a favorite *Annales* word, than it ever had before. Moreover, there is a peculiar advantage that the late sixteenth and the seventeenth century enjoy. In no other field of European history is there so comfortable a balance between paucity and abundance of documentation. With the growth of bureaucracies and the beginnings of parish registration in the sixteenth century, archives become sufficiently rich (at last) to answer most of the major questions asked by modern historians. As the paperwork and its survival rate multiply, however, there comes a point (in most countries around 1700) when the volume of materials starts to cause severe problems of digestion. It may well be, therefore, that only in the early modern period could the type of research done by the *Annales* school have seemed so comprehensive, with such revolutionary consequences for an *entire* subject. Yet, although the reasons for the school's ascendancy may still be conjectural, its effects are unmistakable: a complete rethinking and reopening of topics hitherto regarded as inaccessible or uninteresting, topics which have become the basis for a new synthesis, "a new tradition" and "systematization," to quote Pierre Goubert.[16]

The second major impetus behind the historiographic revival was in some ways an offshoot of the first, and it was again centered on a journal: the English publication *Past & Present*. Founded in 1952 by a group of Oxford and Cambridge dons who seemed to have left-of-center sympathies and interests in social history that were similar to those of the *Annales* school, *Past & Present* rapidly became the liveliest and most provocative historical journal in the English language. And from its earliest days it has placed a heavy stress on sixteenth- and seventeenth-century topics. Throughout its life

16. Pierre Goubert, "Local History," *Historical Studies Today*, ed. Felix Gilbert and S. R. Graubard (New York, 1972), pp. 300–314, esp. pp. 310 and 311. Goubert speaks of "a regeneration of historical studies, with new methods and ideas" (p. 309).

about a third of the scholars on its masthead, and sometimes more, have been specialists in this period—a clearly disproportionate percentage for a general historical journal. And the result, as with *Annales*, has been a quickening of interest in early modern studies, particularly since *Past & Present* has encouraged assertive writing and robust disputes.

Although both the VIe Section and *Past & Present* have been vital stimuli to interest in the late sixteenth and the seventeenth century, it must be admitted that their contribution to the creation of a Europe-wide perspective has been more by implication than example. For both groups continue to concentrate lopsidedly on their own respective countries, a tendency that they themselves have deplored.[17] This narrowness has been less characteristic of *Past & Present*, in whose pages one of the first major efforts was made to see a European-wide pattern for this period. Nonetheless, it seems safe to say that it was a third impetus to the study of the sixteenth and seventeenth centuries that most directly suggested to historians that this era might have an international unity not unlike that of the Reformation or the Enlightenment: the growing study of the history of science.

Here the impetus has been more noticeably American, the result of a very rapid transformation. Until after World War II there was only a tiny handful of scholars interested in this subject—Duhem, Sarton, Koyré, and Merton were the most notable—scattered through various academic departments.[18] By the 1960's there were

17. It is a commonplace, for example, that members of the *Annales* school have restricted themselves exclusively to Mediterranean countries: primarily France, and to a lesser extent Italy and Spain. They have produced no work on northern or central Europe, and in private conversations have often regretted the lacunae.

18. Pierre Duhem, *Le Système du monde* (Paris, 1913-59); George Sarton, *Introduction to the History of Science* (Baltimore, 1927); Alexandre Koyré, *Études Galiléennes* (Paris, 1939); Robert K. Merton, *Science, Technology and Society in Seventeenth-Century England* (Bruges, 1938: vol. IV of *Osiris*, pp. 360-632). One other important contribution between the world wars should be mentioned: E. A. Burtt's *The Metaphysical Foundations of Modern Science* (London, 1924), an influential book which, however, remained much more closely tied to the history of philosophy than the above works. These were not the only scholars working on early modern science—Edgar Zilsel, Charles Haskins, and a number

departments (or at least regular faculty positions) devoted solely to the history or philosophy of science at most major universities in the United States; and, despite the doubts historians of science express about their own influence, it is clear that they have had a considerable impact, particularly on colleagues interested in intellectual history.[19] This is especially true of the sixteenth and seventeenth centuries, the period on which they have spent most of their energies, for the obvious reason that it witnessed *the* Scientific Revolution. Herbert Butterfield's brief survey has had a wide readership, and one reason that specialists in early modern history are now beginning to regard the age they study as a decisive moment in Western history is because of historians of science. If Butterfield could claim that what happened in these centuries was more important than anything that had taken place since the rise of Christianity, then there was more than enough justification for wondering whether other themes not only unified the period but also established its critical importance.[20]

Within a short time just such a set of themes appeared, appropriately promulgated in the pages of *Past & Present*, and made the subject of the first book of essays taken from that journal: *Crisis in Europe, 1560-1600*.[21] Although outsiders might plausibly remain skeptical when pioneers so quickly suggest great significance for their own branch of endeavor, a skepticism perhaps reinforced by the pugnaciousness of the pioneers and their occasional lack of con-

of their contemporaries also ventured into the subject, but none made it a principal focus of his work, and none had a formative influence on the field to compare with the four men mentioned above.

19. The most forceful statement of the doubts is Thomas S. Kuhn, "The Relations between History and History of Science," *Historical Studies Today*, ed. Gilbert and Graubard, pp. 159-92. Yet the infusion of his subject into general history is indicated by the careers of two of his fellow-authors in that volume: Robert Darnton and Frank Manuel. Neither was trained as a historian of science, and yet both have made contributions to that subject, the former through a study of mesmerism, the latter through a major investigation of Newton.

20. Herbert Butterfield, *The Origins of Modern Science* (London, 1949). There have been at least a dozen reprintings since that first edition. On p. 7 of the 1962 Collier edition is the famous remark: the scientific revolution "outshines everything since the rise of Christianity and reduces the Renaissance and Reformation to the rank of mere episodes."

21. Edited by Trevor Aston (London, 1965).

cern for extensive evidence, the "crisis" thesis has in fact received widespread attention and has inspired a great deal of research.[22] In the introduction to the *Crisis in Europe* volume Christopher Hill argued that now "a basis of agreement may have been reached on some features of seventeenth-century history"; while another member of the journal's editorial board, Lawrence Stone, took it for granted, in a long review of the book, that the "crisis" was an established phenomenon, replacing previous interpretations of the period, and that the chief remaining problem was to explain why it happened.[23] Despite some recent doubts about the usefulness of the "crisis" thesis (to be discussed below), Hill's and Stone's confidence does not seem to have been misplaced. The term has found its way into most new textbooks, even when it is not entirely appropriate, and the current generation of students is apparently being taught that the "crisis" can serve as an organizing principle no less powerful than "Reformation" or "Enlightenment."[24]

This, then, has been the principal result of the flurry of work since the late 1940's, both to the profession at large and to specialists. If it can be said to have assured that a holistic approach now reigns—that Spinoza or Masaniello are as integrated into their age as are Erasmus or Müntzer into theirs; that fragmentation and a lack of coherence and clarity have been replaced by a crisp and consistent framework for understanding early modern Europe—few would doubt that the promise of Hobsbawm's original article has been fulfilled. The consequences would be comparable to the

22. See below, notes 24 and 29.
23. Hill in *Crisis in Europe*, p. 3; Stone, "The Century of Crisis," *The New York Review of Books*, VI, No. 3 (1966), pp. 13-16.
24. The most widely used recent textbooks, all of which reflect the "crisis" thesis, are: David Maland, *Europe in the Seventeenth Century* (London, 1966); A. Lloyd Moote, *The Seventeenth Century: Europe in Ferment* (Lexington, Mass., 1970); and Henry Kamen, *The Iron Century: Social Change in Europe 1550-1660* (New York, 1971). This approach has also become standard in even more basic, "Western Civilization," introductory books: for instance, Jerome Blum et al., *The European World: A History*, 2nd edition (Boston, 1970); Shepard B. Clough et al., eds., *The European Past*, 2nd edition (New York, 1970), Vol. I; Charles D. Hamilton, ed., *Western Civilization: Recent Interpretations* (New York, 1973), Vol. I; and J. R. Major et al., *Civilization in the Western World* (Philadelphia, 1967).

achievement of Michelet and Burckhardt in formulating the modern conception of the Renaissance. To see whether the new insights are of this order, however, we must take a closer look at the proponents and critics of the "crisis" interpretation, their accomplishments and failures.

III

PROPONENTS AND CRITICS
OF THE "CRISIS"

Although there are fourteen contributors to *Crisis in Europe*, it is the first two, Eric Hobsbawm and Hugh Trevor-Roper, who lay down the fundamental interpretation which, with variations, underlies the remainder of the volume. Drawing on two areas of research, economic/demographic history and administrative/political history, respectively, Hobsbawm and Trevor-Roper offer two standpoints from which to comprehend late sixteenth- and seventeenth-century history.[25]

For Hobsbawm the fact that the great economic and population boom of the sixteenth century came to an end, to be succeeded by the stagnation and frequent recessions of the seventeenth century, indicated that there was a "crisis" both in the "old colonial system" and in internal production. Wealth had grown too fast, and was put to unproductive uses—particularly by a wasteful aristocracy. The "crisis" brought about a new concentration of capital and cleared the way for the industrial revolution, because Europe's economy was healthier and more "progressive" when it recovered in the late seventeenth century. The implication is that the troubles of the seventeenth century somehow set right what was wrong with the economy in the previous period, removed obstacles, and allowed a new economic situation to emerge around 1700. Viewed from a Marxist standpoint, this transition is presented as a decisive stage in the progression from feudalism to capitalism. Hobsbawm

---

25. *Crisis in Europe*, pp. 5-95. Hobsbawm's article consisted both of the article cited in note 3, above, and of a complementary article in the succeeding issue of *Past & Present*, the consolidated piece in *Crisis in Europe* being entitled "The Crisis of the Seventeenth Century."

only briefly mentioned population, but a lot of the research on which his synthesis is based suggests that demographic stagnation or decline went hand in hand with economic trends.[26] And the take-off of the eighteenth century took place in both areas. We thus have "crisis" as cleanser—the broom that swept away the old and made way for the new.

Trevor-Roper finds the manifestation of the "crisis" in the series of revolts that wracked western European states in the mid-seventeenth century. Nearly forty years ago Merriman pointed to the contemporaneity of revolutions in the 1640's and 1650's.[27] He is hardly mentioned in the *Crisis in Europe* volume, perhaps because he concluded that there were no important common features among the various upheavals, only local conditions. Trevor-Roper's entire purpose is to uncover the links—between Catalan revolt, Fronde, English Revolution, and disturbances in the Netherlands. He finds his organizing principle in the thesis he originally enunciated as an interpretation of the origins of the English Civil War: the struggle between "Court" and "Country." As parasitic, over-loaded central Courts grew, they generated increasing resentment among those left outside the charmed circle, not only because "outs" always dislike "ins," but also because these particular "ins" seemed especially vulgar and distasteful. They were tolerated as long as prosperity lasted—this is the one point at which there is a tenuous link with Hobsbawm's formulation—but in the second quarter of the seventeenth century a new "puritanism" (not a religious doctrine, but an ascetic distaste for Court extravagance) drove an immovable wedge between Court and Country. A violent attack was launched on the Renaissance Court, Society clashed with the State, and the overweening central power was either brought down or, as in France, rationally organized. Amendments to this view have been offered by Roland Mousnier and John Elliott, the former stressing that sometimes in France officeholders themselves rose against the State, and the latter cautioning that the essence of Spain's difficulties was the struggle between peripheral regions and the center, rather than dislike of an overloaded Court.[28]

26. See especially note 5 in *ibid.*, p. 8.
27. *Six Contemporaneous Revolutions*, published in 1938.
28. *Crisis in Europe*, pp. 97-110.

The remainder of the volume, and a series of studies published since its appearance, have added flesh and variety to the "crisis" interpretation, mainly to Trevor-Roper's thesis. The influence of increasingly expensive warfare on the "crisis," and its manifestations in Sweden, Denmark, Ireland, Portugal, Mexico, central Europe, and French finances of the early 1660's have all received attention.[29] And, although Hobsbawm's particular understanding of the collapse of the boom has had fewer echoes, the basic phenomenon he described—economic and demographic slowdown—has continued to inspire a steady flow of research.[30]

Four elaborators or modifiers of the original set of arguments deserve special mention, because they have not only broadened the terms of the discussion but have also highlighted some of its problems. The year after the *Crisis in Europe* volume appeared Ivo

29. Michael Roberts, "The Military Revolution, 1560-1660," in his *Essays in Swedish History* (London, 1967), pp. 195-225, esp. p. 207, and "Queen Christina and the General Crisis of the Seventeenth Century," *ibid.*, pp. 111-37; E. L. Petersen, "La Crise de la noblesse danoise entre 1530 et 1660," *Annales Économies Sociétés Civilisations* (henceforth *Annales*), XXIII (1968), 1237-61; Aidan Clarke, "Ireland and the General Crisis," *Past & Present*, No. 48 (1970), 79-99; Pierre Chaunu, "Brésil et l'Atlantique au XVIIe siècle," *Annales*, XVI (1961), 1176-1207; J. I. Israel, "Mexico and the 'General Crisis' of the Seventeenth Century," *Past & Present*, No. 63 (1974), 33-57; Julian Dent, "An Aspect of the Crisis of the Seventeenth Century: The Collapse of the Financial Administration of the French Monarchy (1653-61)," *Economic History Review*, 2nd series, XX (1967), 241-256, a subject set in a broader context in Dent's *Crisis in Finance: Crown, Financiers and Society in Seventeenth Century France* (Newton Abbot, 1973); and the articles by Polišenský cited below, note 35. The parallels for Scotland have been drawn by David Stevenson, *The Scottish Revolution, 1637-1644: The Triumph of the Covenanters* (Newton Abbot, 1973).

30. The research has been summarized in E. E. Rich and C. H. Wilson, eds., *The Cambridge Economic History of Europe, IV: The Economy of Expanding Europe in the 16th and 17th Centuries* (Cambridge, 1967), esp. on pp. 40-58 of the article by Karl F. Helleiner and in the graphs on pp. 458-85 accompanying the article by Fernand Braudel and Frank Spooner. References to the principal research are provided by Steensgaard in the article cited in note 37, below. Of particular importance is the article by Ruggiero Romano, "Tra XVI e XVII Secolo. Una Crisi Economica: 1619-1622," *Rivista Storica Italiana*, 74 (1962), 480-531.

Schöffer published an English translation of a talk he had first given in 1963, in which he offered a somewhat reluctant endorsement to the "crisis" literature.[31] Paying tribute primarily to Roland Mousnier (to be discussed below), he agreed that the previous "fragmentary treatment" of the period was unacceptable, for "we just simply have to give the 17th century a place of its own."[32] But, despite "the chorus of delight" that had greeted this new organizing principle, he remained dubious: he was uncomfortable with the vagueness of the word "crisis"; concerned that Holland, in its "golden age," was such an exception; uncertain how Baroque art fitted into the thesis; and disturbed at the indeterminacy of the social and economic evidence.[33] He preferred the terms "stabilization" and "shift" to "crisis," for they seemed more descriptive of what he considered the main tendencies of seventeenth-century history: political centralization, the consolidation of the nobility's supremacy, and the solidification of social, economic, and demographic patterns. Although Schöffer's exposition was at a very general level that allowed him little room for detailed analysis or chronological precision, his primary (albeit briefly stated) contention—that there was a gradual "settling down," that life "became more settled and stable"[34]—will be developed into a much-expanded, fleshed-out means of analysis in the pages that follow.

A year later Josef Polišenský undertook a description of recent writings on the Thirty Years' War so as to propose "the conception of the crisis as an aggravation and culmination of the internal contradictions in the structure of a given society or at least in some of its components which brings about a violent impact on . . . economic, social, cultural relations, and has as a result either a regional or general regress or a rapid progress of . . . social development."[35]

31. "Did Holland's Golden Age Co-incide with a Period of Crisis?" *Acta Historiae Neerlandica,* I (1966), 82-107.
32. *Ibid.,* p. 83.
33. *Ibid.,* pp. 86-93.
34. *Ibid.,* p. 106.
35. "The Thirty Years' War: Problems of Motive, Extent and Effect, "*Historica,*" XIV (1967), 77-90. The quotation is on p. 80. Polišenský made much the same argument, more briefly, in "The Thirty Years' War and the Crises and Revolutions of Seventeenth-Century Europe," *Past & Present,* No. 39 (1968), 34-43.

By this standard, he regarded the Thirty Years' War as a "crisis" at least for central Europe and possibly for the entire Continent. Although he offered little evidence outside of Bohemia for the slowdown or acceleration he mentioned at the end of the above quotation (apparently only in England and Holland was the "crisis" positively solved), he did think that " a new conception of civilisation" came into being everywhere around 1600.[36] For all the difficulties of such an interpretation, the notion of "an aggravation and culmination of internal contradictions" has wide applicability, as we shall see.

The first overview of the controversy that was both comprehensive and favorable to the "crisis" thesis was published by Niels Steensgaard in 1970. He feared that the doubts expressed by Schöffer and the stinging attack by A. D. Lublinskaya (see below) had made a "wreck of a debate and a concept that a few years ago looked so promising."[37] Yet he found it impossible to deny that there had been an agrarian and demographic "crisis" in the seventeenth century; the problematical judgments, according to him, centered on industry and international trade, which seemed to resemble a seesaw, not a swing, and therefore revealed no clear trends. To make up for this deficiency, he emphasized the change in public expenditures and taxation. Here a fundamental shift could be perceived, and he suggested "that the seventeenth century crisis from the economic point of view primarily was a shift in demand caused by a transfer of income from the private to the public sector by means of taxation."[38] In this way, too, he could assess the political upheavals of mid-century as a response to government taxation, inherent bureaucratic corruption, and a centrally devised "redistribution of income."[39] Steensgaard's attempt to rehabilitate the "crisis" theory added a new dimension by highlighting the ubiquitous effects of rapid administrative aggrandizement, and by linking them to the economic and political elements of the thesis. There was now

36. *Historica* article, p. 80.
37. "The Economic and Political Crisis of the Seventeenth Century," *XIII International Congress of Historical Sciences* (Moscow, 1970). The quotation is on p. 2.
38. *Ibid.*, p. 5.
39. *Ibid.*, p.7.

an underlying unity that could resolve the disparities among the previous interpretations.

It was in the following year that there appeared the latest and most sweeping effort to pre-empt the hypotheses of the *Past & Present* group by creating a new synthesis. One of the editors of the left-wing *Studi Storici*, Rosario Villari, who had written a monograph on the Naples rebellion of 1647, rejected as politically motivated the approach of Trevor-Roper and Mousnier.[40] "The hypothesis of imbalance between bureaucratic expansion and the needs of the state," he wrote, "is too vague to be plausible, and rests on inflated rhetoric, typical of a certain kind of political conservatism, rather than on effective analysis."[41] He regarded the discontent as a sign, not of imbalance, but of the strengthening of the state. Trevor-Roper's main aim, in his view, had been to attack Marxist historiography by downgrading the Cromwellian revolution, and presumably by implication all the upheavals of mid-century.[42] Villari was equally contemptuous of other "conservative" suggestions: that with greater intelligence rulers could have prevented the troubles; that governments were progressive while protestors were reactionary and bereft of original ideas; that the troubles were merely conspiratorial; or that the aristocracy was a force for change. The last claim Villari dismissed by ignoring Oxernstierna and the first Viscount Saye and Sele, among many others, while emphasizing the nobility's private ambitions and its gradual domestication.

What particularly disturbed Villari was that so few historians seemed willing to recognize "that the revolutionary crisis of the year 1640 was idealistically motivated and had a long and profound

40. "Rivolte e Coscienza Rivoluzionaria nel Secolo XVII," *Studi Storici*, XII (1971), 235-64. His monograph on Naples is *La Rivolta Antispagnola a Napoli. Le Origini, 1585-1647* (Bari, 1967).
41. "Rivolte," p. 240. The original text reads: "l'ipotesi di uno squilibrio tra espansione burocratica ed esigenze dello State è troppo generica per essere plausibile ed è basata piuttosto sull'enfasi retorica, tipica di un certo conservatorismo politico, che su una analisi effetiva." My translation.
42. He sees Trevor-Roper in this regard as coming out of a tradition that started with Gardiner. Equally culpable, in his view, is the historian of Puritan London, Valerie Pearl. *Ibid.*, p. 241 and n.

intellectual preparation."[43] He believed that the movements had grown out of and expanded upon the incontrovertibly idealistic and political aims of late sixteenth-century rebels. Unconvinced by Le Roy Ladurie's dismissal of the "opposition" in Languedoc, he saw in anti-fiscalism—"the *leit motif* of the revolts"—a genuine anti-feudal social movement, reaching its height during the Thirty Years' War, when the derelictions of governments broke all bounds.[44] Indeed, "this great anti-fiscal agitation" was born out of anti-feudalism and a multipronged attack on the class hierarchy, the system of power, the link between government action and economic development, and the functions of the monarchy. In other words, it partook, more concretely than had the messianism or utopianism of the sixteenth century, of social and political revolution. Although Villari sometimes ignored his own warning and relied on rhetoric rather than evidence to establish his case,[45] his revision of the "crisis" thesis does add new bricks to the edifice. One can deplore his ideological attacks on non-Marxists without having to ignore his real contributions: his depiction of the forces and aims that were common even to widely diverse protests; his emphasis on a real exacerbation of tensions and a radicalization of protest as the mid-century approached; and his insistence that the upheavals were centered, not on trivia, but on genuinely far-reaching and significant issues of social and political import.

*   *   *

For all their disagreements, the historians discussed thus far at least seem to be convinced that there was a decisive "crisis" at the heart of the seventeenth century. Those who dissent from this conclusion may be fewer in number, but they have been no less forceful. And they enjoy apparent support from the current leaders of the great tradition of French scholarship that inspired the re-evaluation of the seventeenth century in the first place. I say "apparent,"

---

43. *Ibid.*, p. 253. The original text reads: "che la crisi rivoluzionaria degli anni 1640 ebbe un contenuto ideale ed una preparazione intellettuale lunga e profonda." My translation.
44. *Ibid.*, pp. 258-64. The quotation is from p. 261.
45. He offers no evidence, for example, to justify his equating anti-feudalism and social protest.

because although some of these historians have expressed their doubts in private, they have produced no sustained, explicit refutation. The most that exists in print is a page-long paragraph by Pierre Goubert in which, after repudiating the "crisis" as a "myth," he proceeds to admit that, despite local variations, it might have struck France around 1680.[46] What is more, he restricts his analysis to economic trends, and does not confront the many ramifications of the "crisis" thesis that have now developed. In the absence of more detailed analysis, his comments cannot be said to have posed, on their own, a serious challenge to the *Past & Present* authors and their successors. But another prominent French scholar, Roland Mousnier, has raised a more significant difficulty—not because he has denounced the applications and meaning of the word "crisis," but because he has used the term himself as part of a rather different interpretation of early modern Europe.

Mousnier seemed to be expressing some pique in the *Crisis in Europe* volume when he claimed that, by and large, he had said all these things in a textbook survey published in 1953, a year before Hobsbawm's original article and six years before Trevor-Roper's.[47] At best this is an arguable point, because the one feature that is common to Hobsbawm, Trevor-Roper, and later discussants is the chronology of the "crisis." They all see its origins somewhere around the 1620's, and assume that it was over by the late seventeenth century, with the acute stage passed by the 1660's. For Mousnier, by contrast, western Europe was in perpetual crisis from the beginning of his book (1598) to its end (1715). The nature of the crisis changed from period to period, but the Europeans were never free of it. This is hardly the organizing principle that was suggested by Hobsbawm and Trevor-Roper; nor is it especially useful (in contrast to theirs) as a means of comprehending early modern history. It is too uniform, too undifferentiated, and too lacking in explanatory force. But one of Mousnier's criticisms strikes home quite

46. "Local History," pp. 306-8. He hesitates, however, to dismiss the idea completely.
47. *Crisis in Europe*, pp. 97-98. Mousnier was referring to his *Les XVIe et XVIIe Siècles* (Paris, 1953), Volume IV in *Histoire Générale des Civilisations*, ed. Maurice Crouzet, esp. Book II, all of whose chapters have the word "crisis" in their title.

forcefully, and I shall return to it below—he asks that the analysis not be restricted to the political upheavals of the mid-seventeenth century, but extended to the intellectual, religious, moral, and irrational (i.e., witchcraft) dimensions of the period, which he thinks are connected with the political, though he does not indicate how. Trevor-Roper accepts the validity of the criticism, but again the connections are not pursued.[48]

A much more fundamental onslaught, sparing none of the major "crisis" exponents, has come from a Russian scholar, A. D. Lublinskaya.[49] She clearly believes in no such phenomenon. Her principal targets are Mousnier, Hobsbawm, and Trevor-Roper, and she shows with telling effect that there seem to be more exceptions than rules in their various structures. One of her chief points (and it is one that Schöffer and Stone have also made) is that the economic pattern is in such disarray. The Dutch, for example, achieved unprecedented prosperity during the first half of the seventeenth century, and elsewhere the timing both of decline and of recovery seems totally haphazard. It is a point further reinforced by Goubert, whose contention is that an examination of the localities of France undermines the assumption that any one period was a time of special economic crisis. Bad times came cyclically, and some areas were not hit by real hardship until late in Louis XIV's reign.[50] Lublinskaya also makes the particularly cogent point (and it is not her only one) that Hobsbawm never really indicated how it was that the "crisis" performed its functions. What was the mechanism by

48. *Crisis in Europe*, pp. 103-4 and 115.
49. *French Absolutism: The Crucial Phase, 1620-1629*, trans. Brian Pearce (Cambridge, 1968), esp. pp. 4-102. Widely differing assessments of this book can be found in J. H. Elliott's introduction; G. M. Littlejohn, "An Introduction to Lublinskaya," *Economy and Society*, I (1972), 57-64; and David Parker, "The Social Foundation of French Absolutism 1610-1630," *Past & Present*, No. 53 (1971), 67-89. Lublinskaya's book was first published in Russia, but it was not the first pointed critique of Hobsbawm, having been preceded by six years by F. Mauro, "Sur la 'crise' du XVII siècle," *Annales*, XIV (1959), 181-85. However, Mauro's view, that there was no overall decline because the northern countries benefited from the hardships of the southern countries, has made little impact on the literature.
50. "Local History," pp. 306-8.

which the concentration of economic power and the removal of obstacles to the further growth of capitalism took place? How did the "progressive" win out over the "wasteful?"

She is equally vehement on the subject of the political "crisis." Trevor-Roper's "Court" she calls a meaningless term; England alone, in her opinion, fits his thesis, and badly at that. She admires the various commentators on Trevor-Roper, both in the *Crisis in Europe* volume and in *Past & Present* when his article originally appeared, but that seems to be mainly because they help to weaken his interpretation while offering no alternatives of their own. Particular approval (not undeserved) is bestowed on J. H. Hexter, who attacked Trevor-Roper for making the mid-seventeenth century seem more important than the early sixteenth, and for leaving out science.[51] But she finds everyone at fault (Mousnier as well as Trevor-Roper and Hobsbawm) in their social analysis and in their use of such concepts as mercantilism.

That Lublinskaya exposes serious flaws cannot be doubted. Nevertheless, her conclusion, a barely mitigated plague on everyone's house, is unjustified, especially since her own organizing principle is about as improbable as any that she condemns:

> In the first third of the seventeenth century all the main distinctive features of each of the countries developing towards the bourgeois form of society became clearly outlined. A new "hierarchy" of European states, characteristic of the manufactory period of capitalism and of the early bourgeois revolutions, began to take shape.[52]

If there is any period that seems an unlikely candidate for this bouquet it is the first third of the seventeenth century. A case could be made for any third of the sixteenth century, for the second or the last third of the seventeenth century, or (most likely) for the last third of the eighteenth century. But 1600-1632? The case rests on this being the time when France assumed her role in Europe—a doubtful proposition, for Richelieu did not launch the great attack on the Hapsburgs until 1635—and when England took up her des-

51. *French Absolutism*, pp. 97-98; J. H. Hexter, "Trevor-Roper's 'General Crisis,' " *Past & Present*, No. 18 (1960), 12-18.
52. *French Absolutism*, p. 1.

tiny as the leader of capitalism (far from it, by comparison with the late seventeenth century). Nor is the case strengthened by an almost total indifference to the rest of Europe.

John Elliott, who wrote a foreword to Lublinskaya's book, has emerged as the most penetrating critic of the political "crisis." Not only did he portray Spain as an exception to Trevor-Roper's analysis in the pages of *Past & Present* (on whose editorial board he, too, sits), but he has also made the most incisive statement of the view that the upheaval of the 1640's and 1650's can be regarded as one among many such episodes in early modern Europe. Revolts in this period were relatively limited, he argues, for more serious disturbances had taken place in the 1550's and 1560's. The French wars of religion and the Dutch revolt were much more prolonged and disruptive than anything that happened a hundred years later. Consequently, if economic slowdown and a few simultaneous rebellions were all that could be shown for the seventeenth century, he far preferred to opt for continuity rather than discontinuity.[53]

And indeed, given his terms, Elliott is probably right. If that is all the exponents of the "crisis" can demonstrate, there is little cause to believe they have discovered a vital turning point in European history. But should one abandon the field quite so easily? Is the entire enterprise a chimera because fundamental mistakes were committed, and because by some definitions nothing *did* change dramatically in the mid-seventeenth century? Elliott, for example, considers the decisive advance to have been the metamorphosis of rebellions into revolutions, which did not happen until the late eighteenth century. The "crisis" can thus be dismissed for failing to meet certain familiar criteria, such as "authentic revolution" or "transforming convulsion." But is that the end of the road? The answer must surely be no. So many similar events took place at approximately the same time, in so many areas of Europe and in so many types of human activity—far more than in the mid-sixteenth century—that one cannot escape the impression that something of great importance did in

53. "Revolution and Continuity in Early Modern Europe," *Past & Present*, No. 42 (1969), 35-56. For a pointed criticism of Elliott's views see A. L. Moote, "The Preconditions of Revolution in Early Modern Europe: Did They Really Exist?" *Canadian Journal of History*, VIII (1973), 208-34.

fact take place roughly in the middle third of the seventeenth century. Short of an attachment to coincidences, one is driven to the conclusion that this was the one period between the first three decades of the sixteenth century, the Reformation era, and the last three decades of the eighteenth, the Revolutionary era, when one can speak of a discontinuity. Change was more rapid, extensive, and definitive than at any other time of equivalent length from the 1520's through the 1770's. In attempting to outline the chronological, topical, and causal framework that substantiates this view, I will use the previous literature as a springboard, but the interpretation I will be proposing ranges more widely, and is thus both more hypothetical and sometimes more self-evident.

IV

DEFINING TERMS

The first prerequisite, of course, is to come to terms with the word
that has bedeviled the entire literature: "crisis." Neither Hobsbawm
nor Trevor-Roper thought a definition necessary, and Schöffer, for
one, has pointed out the difficulties they have ignored: the "crisis"
goes on too long, it changes meaning, and it seems no different than
"troubles" in any century.[54] Precise usage presumably requires
conformity to the essential attributes of a word. But tested against
this standard, the scholarship has been woefully inadequate. One
requirement, for example, is that a crisis must be shortlived. Maybe
in historical perspective it can last for a little more than two decades,
as it does in Trevor-Roper's formulation, but it certainly cannot
encompass a century, as it does for Hobsbawm and the title of the
Crisis in Europe book, or even longer, as in Mousnier. Nor can one
evade the problem by suggesting that the "general crisis" was com-
posed of a succession of little "crises," as Mousnier implies. The
phenomenon not only must be shortlived but also—and this is crucial—it ought to be *distinct*, both from what precedes and from
what succeeds.

This second aspect of the definition, the distinctiveness of a
"crisis," is ignored by virtually every contributor to the discussion,
yet it would figure prominently in a purely abstract understanding
of the word.[55] Hobsbawm's schema is the only one that acknowledges this constraint implicitly, for he suggests that the period of

54. "Holland's Golden Age," pp. 86-89.
55. Two excellent theoretical discussions of the term are Oran R. Young,
   The Politics of Force: Bargaining During International Crises (Princeton, 1968) and Randolph Starn, "Historians and 'Crisis,'" *Past & Present*, No. 52 (1971), 3-22. See esp. Young, p. 11, whose theme is that "a
   crisis is usually distinguishable from the pre-crisis and post-crisis period," an idea that is elaborated over the succeeding pages.

"crisis" was different in kind from the age of "seriously wrong" conditions that had been in effect since 1300, and from the era of untrammeled bourgeois society in the early eighteenth century.[56] Trevor-Roper, however, does not really explain (except for England) why the events after 1640 were essentially unlike their predecessors, such as the French wars of religion, and he gives the post-"crisis" era almost no attention. Mousnier apparently finds distinctiveness to be a minor consideration, as do the more recent writers. And when this concern does appear, it almost always takes the form of an interest in antecedents. The denouement is, by contrast, sorely neglected. Even Hobsbawm, one of whose sights is fixed on the future, gives little attention to the question "what came next?" When juxtaposed with the literature's preoccuption with origins, and the lengthy explorations of roots and causes (though not of the differences between cause and event), this omission becomes all the more striking.

The third element in the definition is closely related to the second: a "crisis" cannot merely be distinct; it must also be worse. On this score, none of the proponents of the "crisis" can be faulted. They all agree either that good times turned bad or that a poor situation deteriorated. But of the three attributes of the term this is the least essential. Although there are many ways of describing hard times, only one, "crisis," requires brevity *and* distinctiveness. Without these components, the term becomes downright misleading.

Nevertheless, a concept that has become embedded in historical usage develops a life of its own. To discuss a subject while studiously ignoring the word that commonly describes it is to raise more problems than one solves. Whatever their doubts, scholars and students continue to speak of the Renaissance, the Cold War, and the seventeenth-century "crisis." No amount of debunking is going to remove this shorthand from our consciousness. It is not necessary, however, to surrender to convention without further ado, leaving all the grave reservations intact. Therefore, while retaining the term as part of the following analysis, I will be limiting its application

56. "The Crisis," pp. 5-6.

quite strictly. Circumscribed in usage, it should illuminate rather than befog my purpose.

One attribute of the original (and still most precise) meaning of the word, its medical meaning, stands out with particular saliency, for it is the most familiar and characteristic justification for speaking of a "crisis." Indeed, this is also the one attribute that is unique to the term—namely, that "crisis" is *always* followed by resolution. There are other ways of describing a grave turn for the worse: "paroxysm," for example, refers both to a serious stage of a sickness and to its onset or intensification. But there is no implication that the succeeding stage, subsidence, marks real progress or even the turning point in an illness. Similarly, although "acute" suggests both brevity and severity, it is like "paroxysm" and *unlike* "crisis" in that it fails to suggest that the decisive moment has arrived. One word alone serves that function: "crisis." Whatever follows this stage always represents the final outcome of the pathology, and in fact the phrase most closely associated with the entire sequence is "the crisis has passed." At that point, the outcome becomes clear: the patient either recovers or dies. Which it will be remains uncertain until this moment; but now all doubt is dispelled. By placing the greatest emphasis on the ending—to such a degree that sometimes only the resolution reveals that a "crisis" has occurred—medical practitioners provide the historian with an analogy that can be both specific and fruitful.

Admittedly, this is to take a partial view of the problem; but by restricting oneself to this single (and most crucial) aspect of "crisis" one can at least use the metaphor appropriately and accurately. Since I will be concentrating on "crisis" in relation to its aftermath, I need not make its beginning, intensity, or brevity essential to my definition. Even its distinctiveness will be treated primarily in relation to its sequel. To the extent that, as in medicine, a resolution offers the best proof that a "crisis" has occurred, our evidence of a dividing point will derive mainly from what ensues. For our purposes, therefore, the word will carry none of its broader connotations: it will refer solely to the determinative quality of the period immediately preceding settlement or resolution. I can thus avoid the difficulties that beset Hobsbawm, Trevor-Roper, and Mousnier when they depended on one piece of vague terminology to manage a multitude of heterogeneous events. And I can also draw on different, more appropriate descriptions (such as "rising temperature") for the earlier period, a time of unease and conflict which was certainly rent by disturbance but equally certainly not a "crisis."

Although the word will be limited, in effect, to the divide between turmoil and calm, it is that discontinuity which is the prime focus of this essay. I do not deny that origins and context are important—indeed, they occupy much of the analysis—but they are not so clearly demarcated, and hence require a different terminology. One can distinguish the start of a few particularly acute phases —the English revolution, for instance—but no more than a few, even in politics. Hardly any of the other supposed onsets of "crisis," such as the outbreak of the Fronde in France, would receive general agreement among scholars. Consequently, for reasons of accuracy and appropriateness as well as significance, "crisis" will designate only those upheavals (and implicitly their last, climactic stage) which are followed by a resolution—by an unprecedented appearance of calm and assurance, with an attendant defusing of previous tensions. The change-over may not be immediate. In such long time spans, there is blurring at the edges—or, to use another metaphor, there are after-tremors once the earthquake is over—but the emergence of a new situation is discernible nonetheless.

In another way, too, I intend to depart from earlier interpretations: by insisting that both the rising fever and the "crisis" manifested themselves in almost all fields of human endeavor. Hobsbawm and Trevor-Roper write of a "general crisis," but they seem to mean by the phrase merely that the particular difficulties they stress were experienced by a number of *areas* of western Europe: "general" denotes geographic spread, not the variety of the problems. While its geographic dimension is undeniably pertinent, the "general crisis" would be a more persuasive notion if its generality also reflected a broadened *topical* coverage in which parallels were shared by international relations, painting, literature, religion, and philosophy as well as politics, economics, and demography. For the evidence from the last three is still tenuous enough on its own to warrant doubts about the universality of the argument. Mousnier alone has recognized this shortcoming, but his book treats each "crisis"—in painting, in politics, in science, and so on—as a self-contained entity, one more separate indication that an entire century and a quarter consisted of a "permanent crisis," a "great mutation." The case is built up, not by exposing the uniformity of the phenomenon, but by adding together all the individual "crises," even though most of these specific occurrences are linked with one another simply by the word itself, regardless of the multiplicity of its guises. Yet if the term is to be truly "general" rather than a congeries of particular usages, it must possess some uniformity, and that is the final part of its definition that requires attention.

Can one tell what it was a "crisis" *of?* The feudal-capitalist economy? The Renaissance Court? Ideas and feelings? These are themes that appear in the work of Hobsbawm, Trevor-Roper, and Mousnier, respectively. Along different lines, Steensgaard has highlighted public expenditures and Villari social relations. Yet none of these constructions has relevance beyond one limited area. Moreover, the first three refer primarily to form, not content. They isolate the institution or medium in which the "crisis" took place, not its substance. And although "public expenditures" and "social relations" are indeed *subjects* of conflict, the actual issue remains indeterminate or purely negative: whether the growth of the public sector or the tightening of the social hierarchy will be halted or not. To consider such concrete questions (however important) as the underlying concerns of the time, rather than as symptoms, is to remove the "general" from the "crisis."

What, then, *was* it a "crisis" of? My claim, in a phrase, is that both the rising fever and the final resolution centered on the location of authority. To the question "where does authority come from?" or "what is authentic authority?" there were a number of corollaries: "are there solid and stable certainties?" or "what is order and how certain is it?" or "what is truth and how is it achieved?" or, most extreme, "can one rely on anything?" Throughout these metamorphoses the basic concern remained the same—in a world where everything had been thrown into doubt, where uncertainty and instability reigned, could one attain assurance, control, and a common acceptance of *some* structure where none seemed within reach? When the answer to that sort of question was finally an agreed "yes," particularly among those upper strata that are usually referred to as the "political nation," then the divide had been passed, the "crisis" had been surmounted, and the resolution had arrived. The appearance of the new dispensation, defined in these terms, is essential to my case.

To summarize: since "crisis" must retain its characteristics of brevity and distinctiveness if it is to have any real meaning, I will not be applying it indiscriminately to the mounting tension and conflict of the sixteenth and the early seventeenth century. That will be treated as a separate, preceding stage within the chronological framework—not part of the "crisis," as it is for all previous interpreters. In accordance with the medical model, the break that marks the onset of the "crisis" will not be as crucial as the discontinuity that marks its end. And the succeeding calm will be the chief evidence for the appropriateness of making "crisis" and the passing of "crisis" the central moment, the organizing principle, for some two centuries of European history. Thus it will not be necessary to show that the worst moment in some development came immediately before the resolution; "crisis" is, by definition, the stage directly antecedent to relaxation. My aim will be to show that, despite ups and downs, there was no such relaxation (at least none that was long-lasting and hence genuine) before the middle third of the seventeenth century. Only then did those Europeans who set the tone of their society settle—to their own satisfaction: that is, in *perception* if not always in clear-cut reality—the questions of authority that had been plaguing them for at least a century and a half; only then, with the "crisis" past, could they enter a new era.

With background and definitions in hand, and goals established that are as much heuristic as definitive, we can now try to see if this interpretation of "crisis" lends shape to the early modern period.

V

BEGINNINGS AND
CULTURAL MALAISE

Where to start our story? Almost any time from the fourteenth century on would be appropriate, for the larger development into which our analysis fits is the glacial disintegration of medieval society. Plague, depression, and papal exile and schism were the first devastating blows to that brilliant civilization, and both the fourteenth and fifteenth centuries could be regarded as the seedbed of the disruptions whose resolution we will be examining. But there is no doubt that the sixteenth century witnessed a sharp acceleration of the process of change, and since in any case our main focus will be on a later period, we might as well light upon the incredibly fertile decades around 1500, when one of the major transformations of the Europeans' *Weltanschauung* took place. In fact, there are few generations in Western history when so many new directions were either opened up or fully articulated. The list covers almost every aspect of behavior and thought:

   —In *internal politics*, the beginning of that leap forward in bureaucratization and centralization that used to be associated with the "new monarchs," a term that is now out of fashion but still epitomizes the rapidly growing central governments, and attempts at centralization, that appeared throughout Europe in the last quarter of the fifteenth century and persisted thereafter, fed by the revolution in warfare that took hold at this very time.

   —in *international relations*, the endemic unrest and the new techniques of permanent diplomacy, both of which gained a European-wide dimension in the course of the Italian wars, starting in 1494.

–in *religion*, Luther's protest of 1517.

–in *economics and demography*, the start (probably somewhere in the last quarter of the fifteenth century) of a soaring ascent in population, trade, and eventually prices, symbolized by the accelerating overseas expansion which, between Columbus in 1492 and Magellan in 1519, changed the assumed contours of the world.

–in *intellectual life*, the pragmatism and skepticism of Machiavelli's *Prince*, Castiglione's *Courtier*, Erasmus' *Praise of Folly*, and Copernicus' criticism of Ptolemy, all conceived between 1500 and 1520.

–in *the arts*, the period of the High Renaissance, the culmination of a century-long movement toward idealized, classical perfection, and the first reactions by Mannerists against that ideal.

–in *social relations*, the earliest signs that Europe's traditional localization was breaking down, as central governments impinged on regional authorities, aggressive churches attacked ancient magical beliefs, economic forces stimulated city growth and undermined the tight intimacy of village life, the nobility's preoccupations slowly shifted from countryside to capital, population growth created unprecedented problems, and all these occurrences, together with the multiplication of administrative offices, encouraged a new fluidity and mobility.

Why such a transformation should have taken place is not our present concern. Suffice it to say that the ubiquity and simultaneity of these radical departures stamp the decades around 1500 as a fundamental dividing point in European history. What is vital for our purposes is that the effects of this extraordinary set of changes dominated the Continent for about a century and a half. And indeed, they could hardly have done otherwise, considering the magnitude of the break with the past. There had been foreshadowings in the fourteenth and fifteenth centuries, but not until the decisive decades around 1500 did the new directions become fully apparent, or their consequences so widely felt.

The sixteenth century thus came to be a time of anguished attempts to assimilate and comprehend these strange new forces and ideas. And the disarray, the searching, is dramatically apparent in the culture of the age. For the bewilderment was well-nigh universal, stimulated by shock after shock, and fed and rendered uniform by that great new accelerator of the spread of ideas, printing. In religion, politics, economics, and society, cherished authorities by the score were under attack, and centuries-old values no longer commanded unquestioned adherence. Fanatical self-confidence may have blossomed, but always in opposition to equal fanaticism. Assurance somehow seemed elusive unless it was sustained by blind dogmatism, because single standards were almost nowhere to be found. Catholics, Lutherans, and Calvinists—not to mention the radical sects—clung to irreconcilable world views; overseas discoveries revealed the falsity of ancient geographic assumptions, and brought to light human beings, such as cannibals, whose principles were unthinkable to a European; departures in social, political, and economic affairs changed traditional relationships and institutions beyond recognition: the autonomy of the locality, the supremacy of the aristocracy, and the subservience of the merchant no longer seemed unchallengeable; the mordant cynicism of a Machiavelli and a Rabelais were both symptom and cause of unease; and then Copernicus and Vesalius announced that the descriptions of nature associated with Ptolemy and Galen, which had been revered for over a thousand years, were wrong. No succession of events so disruptive of safe and comfortable suppositions had occurred for hundreds of years. As expectations lost their cogency, an atmosphere of groping and unease descended. Europe's leaders, philosophers, and artists grappled with a world that seemed to be crumbling about them.

The sense that all solid landmarks had disappeared pervades the writing of the age—either because men were toppling the landmarks or because they were seeking them in vain. The contrast between the early sixteenth and the early seventeenth century is especially vivid. Here is Machiavelli, in the unabashed opening sentence of the *Discourses:*

Although the envious nature of men, so prompt to blame and so slow to praise, makes the discovery and introduction of any new principles and systems as dangerous almost as the exploration of unknown seas and continents, yet, animated by that desire which impels me to do what may prove for the common benefit of all, I have resolved to open a new route, which has not yet been followed by any one, and may prove difficult and troublesome, but may also bring me some reward in the approbation of those who will kindly appreciate my efforts.[57]

Against this brash assurance, exuded in a setting whose contours seemed clear though ripe for change, we can set the hesitant probing of an equally profound innovator, Descartes. In the 1610's and 1620's all received standards and all opportunities for progress seemed problematical:

As soon as I had finished the course of studies which usually admits one to the ranks of the learned . . . I found myself saddled with so many doubts and errors that I seemed to have gained nothing in trying to educate myself. . . .

There was no such wisdom in the world as I had previously hoped to find. . . .

I will say nothing of philosophy except that it has been studied for many centuries by the most outstanding minds without having produced anything which is not in dispute and consequently doubtful and uncertain. . . .

Finally, when it came to the other branches of learning, since they took their cardinal principles from philosophy, I judged that nothing solid could have been built on so insecure a foundation. . . .

This is why I gave up my studies entirely . . . [and] resolved to seek no other knowledge than that which I might find within myself, or perhaps in the great book of nature. . . .

Like a man who walks alone in the darkness, I resolved to go so slowly and circumspectly that if I did not get ahead very rapidly I was at least safe from falling. Also, just as the occupants of an old house do not destroy it before a plan for a new one has been thought out, I did not want to reject all the opinions which had

57. Modern Library Edition (New York, 1950), p. 103.

slipped irrationally into my consciousness since birth, until I had first spent enough time planning how to accomplish the task which I was then undertaking, and seeking the true method of obtaining knowledge of everything which my mind was capable of understanding.[58]

And the hesitancy and unease distilled by Descartes provided the impetus for almost every major writer from the mid-sixteenth to the early seventeenth century. The responses were varied, but at their source lay this recognition of disorder and incoherence.

For as the antagonisms, especially religious, but also political and intellectual, became fiercer after the mid-sixteenth century, when the two sides of the confessional struggle coalesced, the obsessive question that began to emerge was the capability of man. On the one hand humanists were orating on his dignity, and they were essentially supported by the Catholics' optimistic teachings on his capabilities and free will. On the other side, however, Luther and Calvin were stressing his innate depravity and helplessness. He could conquer new continents, as Hakluyt trumpeted, but he could not help killing fellow Christians, as Castellio lamented. He could evoke ideal perfection in art through the serenity of a Raphael, but at once he had to cast doubt on that achievement through the distortions of the Mannerists. He could create new wealth and new beggars at one and the same time. These and similar divergences did not escape notice, for they struck at the central issue of man's self-definition. And the means of dealing with such dilemmas were almost as numerous as the issues on which they touched.

Perhaps most significant was the revival of skepticism, which had lain dormant in antiquity, but which aroused new interest in the sixteenth century and experienced a real flowering in the generation of Montaigne and his immediate disciples. It is no coincidence that the organization of sixteenth- and early seventeenth-century thought that most closely parallels my own is in Richard Popkin's authoritative history of skepticism. For the skeptics simply made more explicit and precise what was obviously a basic concern to their contemporaries. And whereas Popkin sees religious antago-

58. Library of Liberal Arts edition, trans. L. J. Lafleur (Indianapolis, 1960), pp. 5, 6, 8, and 14.

nism as the cause of the uncertainty, I see its origins in a broad range
of conflict and change. Yet the end result was the same. So broad
was the impulse toward skepticism, so nagging were the doubts that
it confronted, that even the conqueror of skepticism, Descartes,
seemed, in Popkin's felicitous paradox, "sceptique malgré lui."[59]

For Montaigne was anything but alone in contrasting man's
power and his frailty. The mixture of exhortations to courage—
"there is nothing that throws us so much into dangers as an unthink-
ing eagerness to get clear of them"—and disclosures of weakness—
"I find my opinions infinitely bold and constant in condemning my
inadequacy"[60]—was echoed insistently by the great literature of
his age, not as a standard convention but as a deeply felt concern.
The duality recurs at almost every turn, and Herbert Grierson considered it an essential dichotomy in poetry and drama from Spenser
to Milton.[61] Marlowe's Faust, the very model of universal and brilliant talent, the exemplar of human capacities, sells his soul to obtain
knowledge that is beyond his reach because "Yet art thou still but
Faustus, and a man" (i,i,23). Don Quixote is a treatise on the gap
between hopes and realities, between grasp and reach. And Hamlet
is so painful a figure precisely because he is so remarkably gifted
and vital, yet so helpless in face of the one deed he most wants to
perform. In nearly all of Shakespeare's plays we find ourselves in a
world where the comfortable old values, the traditional verities, are
no longer secure, whether they be the love of a child for its father
or the loyalty of a subject for a king; man, despite his kinship with
the angels, is a quintessence of dust; the time is out of joint. As John
Donne observed, in words that were reminiscent of Hamlet's and
were later to be echoed by Pascal:

> This man, so great, that all that is, is his,
> Oh what a trifle, and poor thing he is.[62]

59. Richard H. Popkin, *The History of Scepticism from Erasmus to Des-
     cartes* (New York, 1964). The designation of Descartes is in the title of
     Chapter X.
60. Michel de Montaigne, *The Complete Essays of Montaigne*, trans. Don-
     ald M. Frame (Garden City, 1960), III, p. 124, and II, p. 366.
61. *Cross-Currents in 17th Century English Literature* (London, 1929).
62. *An Anatomie of the World: The First Anniversary*, lines 169-70. Ham-
     let's "What a piece of work is a man!" speech is an elaboration of the

Nowhere is the disquiet, the evanescence of calm assurance, more apparent than in the dominant forms of painting. Especially by comparison with their immediate predecessors, Mannerists emanated discomfort, imbalance, and restlessness. Nothing seems solid or dependable. The distortions that cast doubt on reality from the work of Pontormo and Parmigianino to the work of El Greco, epitomized by the latter's *Laocoön* (fig. 1) and by Bronzino's *Allegory* (fig. 2); the attachment to "bizarre fantasy"; the obsession with the strained "figura serpentinata"; the disturbing and crammed compositions; the agonies and violent emotions of the subjects; and the impenetrable complexities; all conspired to disturb the viewer, to prevent a contented equanimity. Action was unresolved because, as one scholar has put it, "the tension-free formulae of balance propounded by classical art [were] no longer adequate." Indeed, as the most recent general study of Mannerism has noted, "the threshold of excess was placed abnormally high."[63] So "macabre" were elements of the style, so extreme "the expressive distortion," so strong the "feeling of insecurity," that one art historian has described it as a failure of nerve.[64]

Various efforts have been made to uncover Mannerism in architecture, literature, and music; without extending the inquiry in those directions, however, it is still possible to appreciate the extent to which the taste of the sixteenth century both reflected and encouraged the atmosphere of disquiet that had been engendered by the assault on traditional verities. One need only compare the screaming Magdalen in Titian's *Pietà*, his last painting (fig. 3), or

---

same sentiment, as is Pascal's "What sort of freak then is man! . . . repository of truth, sink of doubt and error, glory and refuse of the universe!" *Pensées*, trans. A. J. Krailsheimer (Baltimore, 1966), p. 64.

63. Arnold Hauser, *The Social History of Art*, trans. Stanley Godman (New York, 1957), II, p. 99. John Shearman, *Mannerism* (Baltimore, 1967), p. 41. See, too, *ibid.*, pp. 22-23, for "bizarre fantasy" and pp. 81-91 (especially Plate 44) for the "figura serpentinata." These books provide excellent illustrations of the style. When, in the remainder of this essay, a specific work of art is referred to but not illustrated, a reference to where an illustration can be found will be given in the Bibliographic Appendix, V.

64. Kenneth Clark, *A Failure of Nerve. Italian Painting, 1520-1535* (Oxford, 1967).

1. El Greco *Laocoön* National Gallery of Art, Washington, D.C.

This painting is indicative not only of the unsettling vision characteristic of Mannerism, but perhaps also of the growing influence of the Counter-Reformation, for it has been suggested that the story of Laocoön, the righteous priest who was ignored and destroyed, might have been an allegory of the dangers faced by the Roman Church.

2. Bronzino *Allegory* National Gallery, London

Mannerist forms are here used differently than in the *Laocoön* (fig. 1)—notably the device of the crammed canvas—but the total effect is similarly unrealistic and unsettling. The subject of the allegory is uncertain, but it may relate to the three stages of life (childhood, maturity, and old age), each of which is represented.

3. Titian *Pietà* Academy of Fine Arts, Venice

Here the unsettlement is personified by Mary Magdalen, on the left, whose fury contrasts sharply with the resignation of the aged St. Joseph, kneeling on the right—a figure thought to be a self-portrait of Titian, then over ninety years old.

4. Michelangelo *Charon's Boat* (detail from *The Last Judgment*) Sistine Chapel, The Vatican

The anguish of the condemned souls on their boat ride to hell typifies the mood of the enormous fresco, painted in the late 1530's, from which this is a small detail.

(Foto Mas)

5. Titian *Bacchanal* Prado Museum, Madrid

This abandoned scene, painted in the early 1520's, some fifty years before the *Pietà* (fig. 3), contrasts in its sunniness with the later work—although, like the Bronzino (fig. 2), it may bear a cautionary message about the three stages of life: the child, the adults, and the old man on his back in upper right.

the tortured soul aboard Charon's boat in Michelangelo's *Last Judgment* (fig. 4), with the languid, powerful figures both these masters had fashioned some years earlier (for instance, in Titian's *Bacchanal* (fig. 5)), to sense the anxiety that had descended on European culture. The phrase with which its historian sums up the archetypal court of the age, that of Rudolf II in Prague, is entirely apropos: it was dominated, he writes, by "the delicate combination of a fatalism about action and a striving for ideal solutions."[65]

Thus far we have been surveying what can be regarded, in terms of our medical metaphor, as the first stage of the illness. The impact of rapid change has made itself felt, and some of the most perceptive and creative minds in Europe have reacted with expressions of doubt, misgiving, and insecurity—emphasizing, in Mannerism as in skepticism, the futility of easy confidence. The old answers no longer work, whether in religion or in studies of nature, but new ones have still to be found. Donne summed up the feeling in a few lines:

> And new Philosophy calls all in doubt,
> The Element of fire is quite put out;
> The Sun is lost, and th'earth, and no man's wit
> Can well direct him where to look for it.
> And freely men confess that this world's spent,
> When in the Planets, and the Firmament
> They seek so many new; they see that this
> Is crumbled out again to his Atomies.
> 'Tis all in pieces, all coherence gone;
> All just supply, and all Relation.[66]

Nor was the sentiment of a Roman Monsignor any different when, in 1616, he heaved a sigh of relief that the Holy Office had declared itself against Galileo's views: "So here we are at last, safely back on a solid Earth, and we do not have to fly with it as so many ants crawling around a balloon."[67] Yet the reactions were not uniform.

65. R. J. W. Evans, *Rudolf II and His World: A Study in Intellectual History, 1576-1612* (Oxford, 1973), p. 274.
66. *Anatomie: First Anniversary*, lines 205-14.
67. Quoted in Giorgio de Santillana, *The Crime of Galileo* (Chicago, 1955), p. 124.

Alongside the feelings of dislocation were vigorous efforts to reassert harmony and control. It is to these that we must now turn, before proceeding to the social, political, and economic developments that were analogues and reinforcements to these trends in thought.

VI

THE FIRST RESPONSE:
CAUTION, ESCAPE, AND CONTROL

One way of coming to terms with the outward disarray was to seek solace within. This was the path taken by the skeptics, as well as by Descartes and Pascal. "In the experience I have of myself," wrote Montaigne, "I find enough to make me wise."[68] And one's self was immediately linked to another source of understanding, Nature. For it was Nature, not the laws of man (or of the Church), which could best provide genuine insights into truth. This was the heart of Bacon's message; this was "the great book" whose perusal Descartes regarded as second only to introspection; and this was the vital stimulus for all the investigations of the scientists. Montaigne distilled the message, and made the connection with the self, in a few brief observations:

> The philosophers with much reason refer us to the rules of Nature . . . [but they] falsify them and show us the face of Nature painted in too high a color, and too sophisticated. . . . As she [Nature] has furnished us with feet to walk with, so she has given us wisdom to guide us in life: a wisdom . . . easy and salutary. . . . The more simply we trust to Nature, the more wisely we trust to her.[69]

The next stage in the argument, which was adopted even by some who placed little faith in Nature, was an insistence on restraint. Knowing one's limitations was essential as a means of resisting the triumph of disorder. It is not surprising that the belief in a Great

---

68. *Complete Essays*, III, p. 319.
69. *Ibid*. The Hermeticists and Paracelsians were also advocates of a return to Nature.

Chain of Being was finally systematized in this period, receiving its
first comprehensive treatment from Leibniz at the culmination of
the Scientific Revolution.[70] For the emphasis on limitation and
moderation was inescapable in philosophic, literary, and above all
scientific statements. "The understanding must not therefore be
supplied with wings," wrote Bacon, "but rather hung with weights,
to keep it from leaping and flying." Newton's "hypotheses non
fingo" derived from similar motives; and, although he had very different reasons, Descartes, too, "resolved to go . . . slowly and circumspectly."[71]

In the theater, just as Marlowe's Faust is destroyed by his pre-
sumption, so the tragic heroes of Shakespeare and the comic heroes
of Molière painfully learn to keep their ambitions and hopes in
bounds. And the last great object lesson in this tradition is Milton's
Satan, banished to hell for overreaching himself. To the extent that
one relies on Nature or the self (and even, in some cases, such as the
Calvinists or the Jansenists, on God's will) to serve as a guide
through the tortuous uncertainties of the world, caution is indispensable. "Greatness of soul," according to Montaigne, "is not so
much pressing upward and forward as knowing how to set oneself
in order and circumscribe oneself. It regards as great whatever is
adequate, and shows its elevation by liking moderate things better
than eminent ones."[72] Over sixty years later he was echoed by
Pascal:

70. Arthur O. Lovejoy, *The Great Chain of Being: A Study of the History
    of an Idea* (Cambridge, Mass., 1936).
71. Francis Bacon, *The New Organon and Related Writings*, ed. F. H. An-
    derson (New York, 1960), p. 98; and see above, note 58. An excellent
    analysis of French classical literature as an attempt to find order amidst
    chaos is Erica Harth, "Exorcising the Beast: Attempts at Rationality in
    French Classicism," *Publications of the Modern Language Association
    of America*, 88 (1973), 19-24. See, too, Albert Guérard, *The Life and
    Death of an Ideal: France in the Classical Age* (London, 1957).
72. *Complete Essays*, III, p. 363. Montaigne's contemporary, the Elizabethan
    composer William Byrd, expressed the same sentiment in a madrigal
    lyric:

    > Extremes are counted worst of all; . . .
    > No wealth is like the quiet mind.

    Edmund H. Fellowes, *English Madrigal Verse* (Oxford, 1967), p. 39.
    The equivalent statement in Molière is put into the mouth of Philinte

I readily consent to being put in the middle and refuse to be at the bottom end, not because it is bottom but because it is the end, for I should refuse just as much to be put at the top.

It is deserting humanity to desert the middle way.

The greatness of the human soul lies in knowing how to keep this course; greatness does not mean going outside it, but rather keeping within it. . . . Nature has set us . . . exactly in the middle.[73]

But these prescriptions were, of course, rarely followed, even by those who wrote them. Scientists themselves, for example, admitted that their subject was also a form of escape from the turmoil of religious and political conflict. Following Bacon's inspiration, the Royal Society determined to exclude all religious or political concerns from its midst ("precluding matters of Theology and State Affairs" in the words of one of its founders, John Wallis), and even the insistence on cautious proceedings and simple, clear language that is so notable in Thomas Sprat's *History* served as a means of setting the members' inquiries off from the turbulence of the world around them. Listing their accomplishments, Sprat noted that "They have attempted, to free [Science] from the Artifice, and Humors, and Passions of Sects." The first meetings of the future Royal Society took place in Civil War Oxford, he explained, because the scientists sought refuge from the "passions and madness of that dismal age."[74] For Descartes, too, the sense of escape was compelling.

Very few could follow the path into natural science, but there were other forms of escape. The remarkable flowering of mysticism in the sixteenth century served this purpose, as it had done in an

---

in *The Misanthrope*: "True reason lies in shunning all extremes; we should be wise in moderation" ("La parfaite raison fuit toute extrémité,/ Et veut que l'on soit sage avec sobriété," I, i, lines 151-52). The entire speech is on this theme—as are most of Molière's plays, at least implicitly.

73. *Pensées*, trans. Krailsheimer, p. 213. This attitude finally triumphed in the era of settlement of the late seventeenth century, when it became a guiding principle of Locke's *Essay Concerning Human Understanding:* "between opinion and knowledge . . . we ought to regulate our assent and moderate our persuasions" (Introduction, para. 3.).

74. The quotations from Wallis and Sprat are cited by Margery Purver, *The Royal Society: Concept and Creation* (London, 1966), pp. 166, 77, and 102.

earlier time of disruption, the late fourteenth century. Its great period lasted until the mid-seventeenth century, often linked with millenarian, messianic, and apocalyptic movements. Even the hierarchically oriented Catholic Church of Spain had to recognize the force of a St. Teresa or a St. John of the Cross; for all the impenetrability of his writings, Jakob Boehme struck a resonant chord among English radicals as well as Silesian mystics; and in Judaism, too, the golden age of cabbalism in Safed, identified with Isaac Luria, and the appeal of Sabbatai Zvi to the imagination of the messianically inclined from Poland to North Africa, betokened a flight to the ineffable that could not be confined.[75] The many apocalyptic and millenarian strivings, which did not die away until the failure of the last major burst of prophecies (centered on the year 1666), derived from similar motives.[76] Indeed, the subsidence of these aspirations was to be one indication that the forces of disorientation had declined, that the "crisis" had passed.

Something of the same character attached itself to the efflorescence of magic and witchcraft: the hopes for easy answers from the astrologer or "cunning man," and for panaceas in the persecution of witches. Here were direct, straightforward means of evading the troubles of the times. But there was another, perhaps more important, aspect to these credulous longings—an obverse that applies equally to the introspection, the reverence for Nature, the self-restraint, the science, and the mysticism and millenarianism mentioned above—and that was the quest for control.

All the themes and manifestations of the culture of the last two-thirds of the sixteenth century and the first third of the seventeenth that we have considered either as a means of escape from, or as an acceptance of, confusion, could also be regarded as desperate attempts to find a new order amidst disintegration. The witches, the astrologers, the alchemists, the hermeticists, the cabbalists, and even

75. This last phenomenon has received definitive treatment in Gershom S. Scholem's magisterial *Sabbatai Sevi: The Mystical Messiah, 1626-1676*, trans. R. J. Z. Werblowsky (Princeton, 1973).

76. Steven Zwicker, "Typology and Prophetic History: The Late Seventeenth Century," unpublished typescript. There is a brilliant examination of the decline of prophecy after mid-century in Elisabeth Labrousse, *L'Entrée de Saturne au Lion: l'éclipse de soleil du 12 août 1654* (The Hague, 1974).

some of the neoplatonists, hungered to find the key that could unlock some all-encompassing secret. They would have access to the true structure of the universe if only they discovered the proper method. For Kepler, the supreme magus of his generation, the hidden harmonies were a life-long goal. And the expectation of all who participated in the search was that magic, properly used, would be an instrument of *control*. Their ultimate aim was to alter or improve the course of nature. They would reveal not only the order that had been lost but also the means of managing it.[77]

Among scientists, often closely related to hermeticists, the ambition to control thought, nature, and "man's estate" hardly requires elaboration. In the midst of doubt and dispute, their target was clear, as even one sentence of Bacon avows:

> Nor is mine a trumpet which summons and excites men to cut each other to pieces with mutual contradictions, or to quarrel and fight with one another; but rather to make peace between themselves, and turning with united forces against the Nature of Things, to storm and occupy her castles and strongholds, and extend the bounds of human empire, as far as God Almighty in his goodness may permit.[78]

The determination to extend "human empire" reflected the most urgent need of an age confronted by dissolving standards of truth and knowledge. Control was the antidote to disarray.

We have seen that various other enthusiasms of approximately the century before the 1650's (such as mysticism and millenarianism) can be regarded, like science, as both escape and instrument of order. But there were some commitments which were more singlemindedly means of regaining control over a refractory world. The first monuments of modern political theory, for example, the works of Bodin and his contemporaries, were attempts to plumb the fundamentals of a relatively new and still mysterious power, the cen-

77. The best introductions to this subject are Frances A. Yates, *Giordano Bruno and the Hermetic Tradition* (Chicago, 1964) and Keith Thomas, *Religion and the Decline of Magic* (New York, 1971).

78. From *The Advancement of Learning*, Book IV, Chapter I, in the translation ed. James Spedding, R. L. Ellis, and D. D. Heath: *The Works of Francis Bacon* (Cambridge, 1863), IX, p. 14.

tralizing territorial state. Different writers naturally forged different implements for mastering this monster, but the basic managerial goal was common to all of them: the revivers of divine right who looked to the holy, anointed king; Bodin, who probed more abstractly into sovereignty; his fellow Roman-lawyers, also enjoying a revival, who supported a secularized version of the divine right monarch; a new breed of historians who ransacked their people's past for guidance in locating authority; and those who had to justify the existence of a minority and fumbled toward a notion of supremacy for the people, or at least for their representatives.[79] The very fertility of political and legal thought in the late sixteenth and the early seventeenth century (accompanied as it was by a breathtaking increase in litigation that produced, for example, a staggering 1500 cases a year in just one English court in the 1610's) indicates how urgently men grappled with the problem of understanding and channelling change. "The worst thing I find in our state," wrote Montaigne, "is instability."[80] It was a conclusion most of his contemporaries would have echoed, and as the conflicts they suffered intensified, so too did their quest for resolution. Not surprisingly, the most radical assessment and proposal of all, Thomas Hobbes' *Leviathan*, appeared when the confusion seemed to have reached its height.

There was a similar blossoming of economic theory in the late sixteenth and the early seventeenth century. Azpilcueta, Bodin, Gresham, Laffemas, the mercantilists—all in their own ways were trying to secure a grip on the bewildering economic torrents of their day. Like the political theorists and the scientists, however, they accomplished nothing for decades except an increase in the occasions and subjects of dispute. Despite the earnestness of their

79. For the literature on political and historical thought, see the Bibliographical Appendix, I. For the figure on court cases cited in the next sentence, and for the enormous growth of legislation in general, see J. S. Flemion, "Slow Process, Due Process, and the High Court of Parliament," *The Historical Journal*, XVII (1974), 3-16, esp. p. 7. The best overall analysis of the rising influence of lawyers is William J. Bouwsma, "Lawyers and Early Modern Culture," *The American Historical Review*, LXXVIII (1973), 303-27, where "law as an antidote to disorder" is discussed on pp. 317 ff.
80. *Complete Essays*, II, p. 364.

endeavors, there was no evidence that they were capable of restoring stability or calm. And the same was true, not only of the battling religions, but also of their philosophical schools. While Catholics returned to neoscholasticism, Protestants turned to Ramism, yet neither doctrine produced a convincing epistemology. For that we have to wait until the "crisis" comes and goes a century later.

The most striking evidence of the belief in knowledge as an agent of comprehension and thus of control was the extraordinary migration into higher education. Lawrence Stone has called this an "educational revolution" in England, and it had its equivalents elsewhere. Over a dozen new universities were founded on the Continent in the second half of the sixteenth century, while the number of students (predominantly aristocratic or close to that status) may have more than doubled. Many reasons have been given for this unprecedented influx—the changing self-definition of the nobility and the influence of Protestantism seem to carry the most weight—but behind them all lay the conviction that, as Marlowe's Faust realized, knowledge is a prerequisite for control: order emerges from comprehension. If Castiglione's precept, "I would have [the courtier] more than passably learned in letters, at least in those studies which we call the humanities," had been their only guide, the aristocracy and well-to-do might not have flocked so abundantly to colleges and universities. The essential additional motive, in Stone's view, was that thereby "they fitted themselves to rule in the new conditions of the modern state," or at least they *thought* they did.[81]

81. J. H. Hexter, "The Education of the Aristocracy in the Renaissance," in his *Reappraisals in History* (Evanston, 1961), pp. 45-70; Lawrence Stone, "The Educational Revolution in England, 1560-1640," *Past & Present*, No. 28 (1964), 41-80; Hugh Kearney, *Scholars and Gentlemen: Universities and Society in Pre-Industrial Britain, 1500-1700* (London, 1970); François de Dainville, "Effectifs des collèges et scolarité aux XVII et XVIII siècles dans le nord-est de la France," *Population*, 10 (1955), 455-88, and "Collèges et fréquentation scolaire au XVII siècle," *ibid.*, 12 (1957), 467-94; Henry Kamen, *Iron Century*, pp. 284-97: "The European Universities," and the literature he cites on pp. 446-47. Faustus' words are: "O, what a world of profit and delight, Of power, of honour, and omnipotence, Is promised to the studious artizan! [namely, to the master of the highest arts]": *Doctor Faustus*, I, i, 54-56. See, too, Baldesar Castiglione, *The Book of the Courtier*, trans. C. S. Singleton (Garden City, 1959), p. 70.

6. Rubens *The Apotheosis of James I* Banqueting House, London

The entire ceiling, which is decorated with eight canvases in addition to this one, is devoted to allegorical glorifications of the benefits James bestowed on his subjects.

7. Rubens *The Marriage of Henry IV and Marie de' Medici* Louvre Museum, Paris

Notice the peacocks, symbols of Juno, which accompany Marie; her husband Henry, of course, appears as Jupiter.

They were hoping to master the world around them, but only as long as it seemed to need mastering. Once the questioning ended, as it did with the "resolution" of the mid-seventeenth century, the tide of matriculants receded almost as quickly as it had risen. Knowledge was apparently no longer needed.

There was one final conspicuous feature of the cultural reaction to the upheavals set in motion in the early sixteenth century. After 1600 the efforts to re-establish a sense of stability and confidence entered a stage of ever more intense striving, of epic enterprises. Again the most immediate evidence comes from painting, where the birth of the Baroque epitomized the belief that grandeur and immensity could subdue uncertainty. Gone was the unsettling vision of Mannerism; in its stead arose a direct, powerful, and unashamed affirmation of emotion, often encouraged by Counter-Reformation Catholicism, that was the visual equivalent of religious and political authoritarianism. Not unexpectedly, its greatest figures—Rubens, Velázquez, Bernini, Borromini—served and apotheosized the monarchs and popes who claimed, with fluctuating success, to be the repositories of all authority. It was precisely because the assertion so often sounded hollow that it was so grandiosely promulgated. Rubens' glorification of the Zeus-like James I in the Banqueting House (fig. 6), or of the Junoesque Marie de' Medici in the Louvre (fig. 7), elevated clearly unsuitable subjects to heroic proportions.[82]

The colossal scope, the vast canvas, was part of an aesthetic that overwhelmed its subject, that silenced doubt, by sheer magnificence and sweep. The profound searchings and awe-inspiring structures devised by Europe's greatest minds during the half-century starting approximately in the 1610's have never been equaled as a concurrence of audaciously sustained confrontations with the basic questions of human existence and confidence. Crammed into a few decades are dozens of farflung intellectual systems, including those of Bacon, Descartes, Spinoza, and Hobbes, alternately hopeful and de-

---

82. Amidst the enormous literature on the Baroque, one article by a historian deserves particular mention, because it does attempt to link the style to broader social problems, including the "crisis": Robert Mandrou, "Le Baroque européen: mentalité pathétique et révolution sociale," *Annales*, XV (1960), 895-914.

spairing about man's possibilities. On an equally imposing scale are not only the paintings, sculptures, and buildings of the period's towering artists but also the more personal searches of a Rembrandt, a Calderón, a Pascal, and a Milton. Each was capable of intimate, tender emotions, but each was also driven to immense outpourings of profound passions monumentally conceived. On every side there is evidence of a deeply felt urge somehow to conquer the truth, to defeat irresolution with an onslaught of prodigious ambition, to convince by sheer temerity and reach. When that kind of aspiration lost its centrality in European culture, as it did from the 1660's on, one could tell, yet again, that the uncertainties and thus the "crisis" had been left behind.

VII

DOMESTIC POLITICS

The intellectual and artistic response to the destruction of traditional authorities, values, and assumptions—its doubts, evasions, and attempts at control—found both a counterpart and a stimulus in other areas of human activity. Although the writers and painters give the most vivid insight into the times, their inspiration came from the equivalent tendencies in political, economic, and social development. For it was here, most of all, that stability proved elusive from the early sixteenth century through the mid-seventeenth century, as new forces were unleashed, conflict and disruption became endemic, and resolutions remained temporary despite the most earnest of intentions. In politics especially, the upheavals and the search for new answers were experienced by every state in Europe.

Common to every kingdom, principality, and republic were certain essential changes in the institutions and aims of politics, many of which aroused fierce opposition. The all-pervasive issue was the increase in central governmental power, exemplified by the growth of bureaucracies. The infiltration of these multiplying public servants into regions and activities that never before had tasted their presence was met by stiffening resistance, primarily from nobles who quickly recognized the threat to their power base in the localities. And the chief instrument, both of the weakening of local lords, and of the proliferation of bureaucrats, was warfare. The compelling needs of the dawning age of gunpowder, first fully felt in the decades around 1500, had dramatic consequences. The vastly increased expense of casting cannon, manufacturing guns and projectiles, and supplying the larger manpower that was required to make effective use of the new technology, put a premium on the resources only a centralized government could marshal.[83] The

83. See the first article by Roberts cited in note 29, above; J. H. Elliott's

provincial aristocrat was incapable of competing and thus of preserving his independent influence. Moreover, the military revolution had spiraling effects. It demanded additional funds, hence higher taxes, hence more bureaucrats to collect and administer the income, hence more salaries, and so on. Each twist in the vicious circle enlarged central governments, and it is significant in this regard that the pressures were not quite as intense in England, the country least involved in the land warfare of the age.

The research has not been done to establish what proportion of Europe's population in 1520 and in 1670 was employed in a centralized bureaucracy, but it would be very surprising if the *percentage* did not at least quadruple (and this in a period when the population itself perhaps doubled). No other conclusion is possible, even from the little that we know about the consequences of Charles V's reforms in Spain, the appearance of the *noblesse de robe* in France, and Thomas Cromwell's "revolution" in England. The tax burden per capita probably did not rise quite as fast, but again one's estimate must be that it at least tripled—the French *gabelle* once tripled in twelve years alone, and even England, least affected by dizzying taxes, witnessed very rapid increases in customs duties, arbitrary exactions, the spoils of office (all common on the Continent, too) and the value of subsidies (when granted) during the late sixteenth and the early seventeenth century.[84] Symbolized by burgeoning incomes and bureaucracies, the spectacular growth of central powers, particularly in the three kingdoms of Spain, France, and England, was not merely an ambitious dream, but a reality that subjects could perceive. No century and a half in European history is as full of great ministers who were also innovative bureaucrats—de los Cobos, Cromwell, the Cecils, Oldenbarne-

comments in *Crisis in Europe*, pp. 105-9; and John Lynch, *Spain under the Habsburgs*, II (Oxford, 1969), pp. 79-86.

84. J. H. Mariéjol, *La Réforme et la Ligue—l'Édit de Nantes (1559-1598)*, Vol. I, Part I of Ernest Lavisse, ed., *Histoire de France* (Paris, 1904), p. 231; R. Doucet, *Les Institutions de la France au XVIe siècle* (Paris, 1948), II, p. 587; F. C. Dietz, *English Public Finance, 1558-1641* (New York, 1932): J. H. Elliott, *Imperial Spain, 1469-1716* (New York, 1964), pp. 193-96 and 279-81; and Lynch, *Spain under the Habsburgs*, I (Oxford 1965), pp. 128-34, and II, pp. 30-39 and 79-93.

velt, Sully, Cranfield, Olivares, Oxenstierna, Richelieu, and Colbert. The process of bureaucratization and the rise of taxes have continued, of course, until our own day, and most people have remained unhappy about both. But the unhappiness is as nothing compared with the distress and dislocations that were caused when the first enormous leap took place. After all, human beings eventually become inured to persistent discomfort: by 1789 Franklin could make his famous remark about the certainty of death and taxes, and sixty years later Dickens' Mr. Barkis agreed that "there's nothing truer than taxes." In the sixteenth and seventeenth centuries, by contrast, a distant government's threat to local independence, and particularly to the powers of the nobles who had always dominated the localities, attained a suddenly unprecedented scale and hence was cause for deep disturbance and violent resistance. Even as mild an attempt at centralization as that conducted in the Empire by Maximilian I and Berthold of Henneberg between 1495 and 1512 suffered immediate rejection and a quick demise.[85]

The decades from the 1520's until the 1660's, therefore, experienced the most sustained and tense phase of the long-standing conflict between, on the one hand, kings, princes, and rulers of states, and, on the other hand, hitherto relatively independent nobles and localities. What is crucial, as far as this period of "rising temperature" is concerned, is that none of the tensions and uncertainties about the basic political system of the individual states of Europe was settled to general satisfaction, or for more than a few tentative decades, until the mid-seventeenth century. Therein lies the principal reason for suggesting that the events of the 1550's and 1560's, whose significance Elliott emphasized, failed to produce decisive, long-term consequences to match those that were achieved one hundred years later. Before the latter period, the future and structure of central governments, and above all their relations with other loci of political power—mainly the upper classes, though sometimes also cities and the Church—were never acceptably decided. Stability might be achieved for a while, but no new framework emerged that was sufficiently final or long-lasting to be free from renewed and

85. Hajo Holborn, *A History of Modern Germany: The Reformation* (New York, 1959), pp. 39-46.

widespread challenge for as long as a hundred years. Not until the mid-seventeenth century could any European state enjoy such luxury.

*   *   *

For Spain, France, and England, the case is quite straightforward. In Spain the question was not so much whether nobles would acquiesce to a centralization that, on the whole, increased rather than diminished their powers, but whether the other provinces would accept the pre-eminence of Castile. From the time of the Catholic Kings, when the Castilians refused to disguise their contempt for Ferdinand of Aragon, through the *comuneros* and the Castilian dislike for the Burgundian Charles V, localism, particularly the opposition of Castile versus the rest, dominated this vast empire. Late in Charles' reign, and during the first half of Philip II's, a measure of unity was attained, particularly when the Castilians were at last satisfied by a monarch, Philip, who was one of their own. But then the troubles began to come from the other direction. Starting with de los Cobos, and increasingly under Philip, Castile had gained importance at the expense of the other provinces. The revolt of the Netherlands was thus primarily a test of whether provincial autonomy (including in this case the powers of local nobles) would be respected by the Castilian centralizers. The first troubles in Aragon began to appear when it emerged that the test was not working in favor of the provinces. The Aragonese revolt of 1591-92 was the prelude to a gradual tightening of tension, exacerbated by worsening economic conditions, until the great onslaught on Castile from Catalonia, the Netherlands, Portugal, Sicily, and Naples reached a shattering climax in the 1640's.

Only when this round was over (with the recognition of Dutch and Portuguese independence, the subjugation of Naples and Sicily, and the conquest of Barcelona) did the final shape of Spain's battered empire begin to become clear. It had to suffer one last assault, the Catalan rebellion of 1705-14, ended by another conquest of Barcelona, but this was an echo, an after-tremor, of the earthquake at mid-century. Castilian hegemony in its old form had disappeared by the 1660's, and the War of Spanish Succession merely confirmed that the outcome was a genuinely centralized state, run by an aris-

tocracy in government service, not a revival of provincial autonomies. What is especially important is that, after some 150 years of
dispute, the structure of politics was now set for centuries.[86]

In France, foreign war, while demanding more bureaucrats and
taxes, diverted the Crown's most dangerous opponents, the nobles,
until the 1560's. Then, however, they started what was probably
the most continuous attack on the monarchy and its powers that
any aristocracy attempted in these years. The vehemence declined
after the first and most virulent phase, up to the 1590's, but it is
hard to avoid the impression that periods of calm were the exception rather than the rule until the end of the Fronde in 1653. In the
interim, Henry IV exercised firm control for about twelve years,
and Richelieu was reasonably well in command for about thirteen
years; yet these were but twenty-five out of some ninety years
when the nobles were seriously testing the authority of the central
government. And they were joined not only by those who felt a
loyalty to a region such as Britanny (though this regionalism was
not as powerful as in the Spanish Empire) but also by peasants,
whose almost annual revolts reflected an increasing distaste for the
activities of the central government. The first wave of peasant uprisings, from the 1520's to the 1550's, was inspired mainly by religious changes; the second, from the 1570's to the 1590's, lashed out
at all sides involved in the devastations of the wars of religion; but
the third and most destructive, from the 1620's to the 1640's, was
directed at tax collectors and bureaucrats—"mort aux gabelleurs,"
they cried.

Before the Fronde was over, therefore, it could not be said that
the growing powers of the central government were generally and
widely accepted, or that Frenchmen considered further resistance
to be pointless. But after the 1650's there could be no doubt. Although a final wave of peasant revolts did not die out until 1675,

86. The principal general works from which this outline emerges are:
Lynch, *Spain under the Habsburgs;* Elliott, *Imperial Spain* and *The Revolt of the Catalans. A Study in the Decline of Spain (1598-1640)* (Cambridge, 1963); and Henry Kamen, *The War of Succession in Spain 1700-
15* (Bloomington, 1969). For the mid-seventeenth century revolts against
Castile, see, too, Villari, *Napoli,* and H. G. Koenigsberger, "The Revolt
of Palermo in 1647," in his *Estates and Revolutions: Essays in Early
Modern European History* (Ithaca, 1971), pp. 253-77.

and a few voices in the wilderness questioned the monarchy, the situation was transformed. The nobility was domesticated, reliant for power on the king, not on its strength in a locality. Condé, still treasonous during the Fronde, ended his days rowing ladies on the lake at Versailles. Camisards and occasional protesters might cause trouble, but nobody seriously challenged the authority of the royal government or its bureaucrats for over a century. In this respect the situation that took hold under Louis XIV, reinforced by a standing army that grew to 400,000 men, was radically different from the starts and stops in the movement toward unquestioned central authority under Francis I, Henry IV, or Richelieu. And, as in Spain, the rising in the Cevennes between 1702 and 1710 was an aftertremor that did not betoken a renewal of the volcanic activity that had been so dangerous until the middle of the seventeenth century. What is especially remarkable is that the grievous famines and depressions of 1693-95 and 1709 produced almost none of the outbursts that would have been expected sixty years before, and that the royal minority after Louis XIV's death had none of the destructive consequences of the minorities of the 1610's and 1640's. The *ancien régime*, as a system, was triumphant and secure.[87]

The English crescendo was more gradual and the climax more evidently a dividing point. But again the period of real security, when the uneasy relations between Crown and nobles and gentry were relatively calm, lasted only for a short while after 1529, when Henry VIII's centralization began to accelerate—mainly the middle years of Elizabeth's reign and the brief honeymoon at the beginning of James I's reign. Wallace MacCaffrey has recently shown, in a study of the 1558-72 period, how delicately poised even Elizabeth's strength was until the execution of the Duke of Norfolk in 1572, a measure whose severity was dictated by the precariousness of the Queen's authority. Thereafter the peers were no longer the chief threats to central power, but the gentry, increasingly active in politics, and openly trespassing on royal prerogatives through the House of Commons, maintained the pressure on the government. Of course there was a huge distance between a Peter Wentworth or an Edwin Sandys, with their essential respect for the throne, and an Oliver

87. For the chief literature on political stability and revolts in France, see the Bibliographic Appendix, II.

Cromwell, as there was also a basic difference between the Arago-nese revolt of 1591 and the Catalan revolt of 1640, or between the French religious wars and the Fronde. But a fundamental unity persisted.

In England that unity can be seen in the determination of those members of the upper classes who dominated the various localities (usually counties) not only to limit the encroachment on their in-dependence and influence that resulted from the government's growing demands (such as its revival of feudal rights), but also to make sure that they themselves had a say, through Parliament, in what that government was doing. The collision between these am-bitions and the very different aims of the monarchy was virtually continuous from the 1530's, despite variations in its forms and mag-nitude. Admittedly, the movement toward an open break began to gather force only in the increasingly hostile parliamentary sessions of the early seventeenth century; nevertheless, the eruption of 1640-60 took place over issues that Wentworth or Edward Coke would have recognized—how far does central power extend, and what autonomies are reserved to those who are great men in the localities?[88]

Moreover, the revolution's accomplishment was not a series of great changes but precisely the conclusion of these old and bitterly disputed questions. To that extent the outcome paralleled exactly

88. Wallace MacCaffrey, *The Shaping of the Elizabethan Regime* (Prince-ton, 1968); J. E. Neale, *Elizabeth I and Her Parliaments* (London, 1953-57); Wallace Notestein, *The Winning of the Initiative by the House of Commons* (London, 1924); Margaret A. Judson, *The Crisis of the Con-stitution: An Essay in Constitutional and Political Thought in England 1603-1645* (New Brunswick, N.J., 1949); Perez Zagorin, *The Court and the Country* (London, 1969); Lawrence Stone, *The Causes of the English Revolution, 1529-1642* (New York, 1972); and Christopher Hill, *The Century of Revolution, 1603-1714* (Edinburgh, 1961) are the stand-ard works on these political developments. For a useful recent discussion of general interpretations, see the debate betwen H. G. Koenigsberger and Lawrence Stone in *The Journal of Modern History*, 46 (1974), 99-110. A book that reached me only when the present work was in press, D. M. Loades, *Politics and the Nation, 1450-1660: Obedience, Resistance and Public Order* (London, 1974), provides a good introduction to the issue of political authority and how it was viewed and experienced by England's elite during this period.

the settlements in Spain and France.[89] And in England, too, there was one more test, a last tremor, before the challenges died away. Yet the very ease with which the threat of James II in the 1680's was surmounted revealed the firmness of Englishmen's belief that they had put behind them the problems he raised. The new system was in place: seemingly clear after 1660, and irrevocably clear after 1690, was the fact that men of property, through their instrument, Parliament, possessed the share in central authority that the Crown had denied them.[90]

One general characteristic of these developments ought to be noted at this point. The resolution of a century and a half of doubt and tension did not mean that the shape of a long-emerging political structure now had to change—a particular momentum might be reversed or it might be confirmed. In other words, the specific form that a political system eventually assumed (absolutist, aristocratic, or mixed) was less important than the fact that *now it seemed settled*. What distinguished it from its pre-resolution incarnation was that, at last, it remained free from serious threats of major transformation for at least a century.

Elsewhere in Europe one finds the same kind of problem and a similar progression. Within the United Provinces the great issue

89. Since by no stretch of the imagination could one designate the upheavals and settlements in Spain and France as revolutions, there may be good reason to doubt whether the similar English troubles, with their similar consequences, should be called a revolution. Further discussion of this issue, in a broader context, can be found in Robert Forster and Jack P. Greene, eds., *Preconditions of Revolution in Early Modern Europe* (Baltimore, 1970); Stone, *Causes;* the article by Moote cited in note 53, above; and Martha François, "Revolts in Late Medieval and Early Modern Europe: A Spiral Model," *Journal of Interdisciplinary History,* V (1974), 19-43.

90. The most recent study of this subject, J. H. Plumb, *The Growth of Political Stability in England 1675-1725* (London, 1967), argues that the process was not complete until the rise of Walpole, but admits that after the overthrow of James II "few could dispute where sovereignty ultimately lay"—namely, the Commons. (American edition, Baltimore, 1969, p. 73.) See, too, Daniel A. Baugh, "The Modernization of Bureaucracy in Eighteenth-Century England in the Context of Three Centuries" (unpublished typescript), which points to the late seventeenth century as the time when the structure coalesced.

was whether the House of Orange, standing for political consolidation, war, and religious orthodoxy, or some more decentralized structure based on the seven provinces, especially Holland, representing peace, religious pluralism, and commerce, would emerge as the dominant force in the government. Although each side had its successes and failures, the issue was not completely resolved in favor of the final compromise between the two sides until the murder of Jan de Witt, Holland's Grand Pensionary, in 1672. During the two decades of his rule the future direction of the country still seemed in the balance, but after 1672 the rivalry between Holland and Orange waned, even when William III died and one might have expected Heinsius to act as a new Oldenbarnevelt or Witt.[91]

In the Holy Roman Empire the authority of the Emperor vis-à-vis the princes, and that of the princes vis-à-vis their subjects, was a matter of chronic dispute that again lost its potency in the mid-seventeenth century. Charles V's and Ferdinand II's campaigns, in the 1540's and the 1620's, to establish control over the vast territory that legally owed them allegiance, were merely the most violently opposed of the persistent efforts to dominate Germany's princes from Vienna. Imperial ambitions and local resistance were sources of endemic strife that did not come to an end (despite the Treaty of Prague) until the Peace of Westphalia and Leopold I's *Wahlkapitulation* finally recognized the princes' independence. Nor was it apparent until the second half of the seventeenth century that the Hapsburgs had finally subdued noble opposition within their own territories (especially Bohemia, which was not pacified until the 1650's), or that their ambitions now extended along the Danube rather than the Rhine. Moreover, like rulers elsewhere, they survived without difficulty the final tests of their authority—the siege of Vienna in 1683, and peasant revolts in Hungary and the Tirol at the end of Leopold's reign—because their ascendancy was now secure.[92]

91. The basic source remains Peter Geyl, *The Netherlands in the Seventeenth Century*, 2nd edition (New York, 1961-64). See, too, Herbert H. Rowen, "The Revolution That Wasn't: The *Coup d'État* of 1650 in Holland," *European Studies Review*, 4 (1974), 99-117.

92. The standard account is Holborn, *Germany*. See, too, Bruno Gebhardt, ed., *Handbuch der deutschen Geschichte*, Vol. II (Stuttgart, 1955), and John Stoye, *The Siege of Vienna* (London, 1964).

And the relations of the German princes with their own nobles and Diets repeated in miniature, especially in Brandenburg-Prussia, what was happening in larger territories—a long struggle, with the form of the government settled, for at least a hundred years, in the middle third of the seventeenth century. If, in the process, the trend was toward consolidation (an aspect of centralization that spelled doom for such anomalies as imperial knights and free cities), that does not mean that the outcome was always in the prince's favor. The structure was established, and was not significantly endangered until the Napoleonic conquest, but authority could go either way— to Württemberg's powerful Diet or to Brandenburg-Prussia's Elector and Junkers.[93]

Scandinavia went through the same fumbling toward settled forms of government. Sweden's assertion of independence from Denmark in 1523 was a reaction by a region and its leading nobles against the intrusions of Christian II, the king in Copenhagen. For the next century and a half, however, the Vasa dynasty, too, had to work out, very gradually, its relations with its nobles. The role of the grandees was the main problem until the beginning of Gustavus Adolphus' reign in 1611, when the principal aristocrats were soothed by incorporation into the central government; during the next few decades there were moments when Sweden looked like an oligarchy. But in 1650, according to Michael Roberts, "the monarchy begins to swap horses," and by 1680 the Crown's alliance had been transferred from the high nobles to the lesser nobles. The one major difference between Sweden and other states is that its final structure was achieved under moderate pressure and without the violence of the Empire, France, Spain, England, and even the Netherlands. Nevertheless, a century and a half was needed to dispel the uncertainty of the eventual outcome, a settlement which, as elsewhere, survived one final challenge unimpaired—in this case the strains of Charles XII's last years and the period immediately following his death.[94]

93. See F. L. Carsten, *Princes and Parliaments in Germany from the Fifteenth to the Eighteenth Century* (Oxford, 1959).
94. Michael Roberts' various works cover all aspects of this period: *The Early Vasas: A History of Sweden 1523-1611* (Cambridge, 1968); *Gustavus Adolphus: A History of Sweden 1611-1632* (London, 1953-58);

The Danish pattern was almost a classic example of the struggles of the time. Following Swedish independence in 1523, a civil war broke out which pitted the bulk of the nobility against the king and his allies, drawn mainly from non-aristocrats. Order was restored in the mid-1530's, and the monarchy gradually managed to extend its power during the next century in the face of substantial but ultimately ineffective noble discontent. When the most powerful of the kings, Christian IV, died in 1648 at the end of a sixty-year reign, the aristocracy's unhappiness turned to action, and a coup gave it virtual control of the government. Not until 1660 could the new king, Frederick III, turn the tables and establish an absolutist system of government, based on an alliance between Crown and townsmen, that was not again questioned for over a century.[95]

Although my interpretation relates primarily to western and central Europe, the parallels further east are certainly striking. The first use of a single *liberum veto* to paralyze the Polish Diet, the Seym, in 1652, and the rebellions of Khmelnitsky and Stenka Razin, all in their own ways resolved long-standing problems of political structure—finally dooming Poland to aristocratic anarchy, bringing the Ukraine under Moscow's domination, and removing the last obstacle (the Cossacks) that might have limited Peter the Great's autocracy. Whereas the solution to the problems of authority that had been endemic at least since the reign of Sigismund III in Poland and the Time of Troubles in Russia could have gone in any one of a number of directions, by the last third of the seventeenth century only a single path remained. Interestingly enough, the most recent historian of the subject attributes the rigidification of Russian society and the conclusive establishment of serfdom in the 1640's and 1650's to the rising needs of warfare.[96]

*   *   *

---

and *Essays in Swedish History*, cited in note 29, above. The quotation comes from the latter, p. 126. See, too, R. M. Hatton, *Charles XII of Sweden* (London, 1968), which stresses the King's role as the defender of Gustavus Adolphus' heritage rather than as an innovator in foreign or domestic policy.

95. See the article by Petersen cited in note 29, above.

96. Richard Hellie, *Enserfment and Military Change in Muscovy* (Chicago, 1971).

Considerable space has been given to internal developments within each of the states of western Europe not because politics is innately more important than such topics as international relations, religion, or art, but because this is the area in which the pattern is most in need of demonstration (especially if it is to be called virtually European-wide) and because, once established, it displays the outline of the argument most clearly. The thesis can now be described quite simply. Throughout Europe states had to grapple for more than a hundred years with forces that were set in motion at some point in the half-century around 1500. The underlying impetus was provided by the ambitions of central governments, usually fueled by the needs of warfare. The expansion of bureaucracies and taxes, and the general interventionism (for example, the beginnings of widespread attempts to centralize justice, poor relief, economic regulation, military organization, and political control), were pursued entirely at the expense of provincial autonomies and aristocratic privileges. Naturally, those who felt put upon struck back as hard as they could—the cities, the previous seats of economic regulation, could not resist very effectively, but the provinces and aristocrats could. As a result, the ultimate balance between central and regional authority, and between dynastic, monarchical, or princely power and noble power, remained uncertain. The struggle over that balance continued, on and off, and in varying degrees of intensity, until the mid-seventeenth century. Sometimes the earlier explosions were much more violent than the later—as in France— and sometimes not—as in England. What is essential to the analysis, however, is that in no case was the situation pacified, freed from a renewal of conflict every few decades, until the middle of the seventeenth century, when the problems ceased to polarize society for over a hundred years.

Whether the issues had really been settled, or whether the various groups simply stopped squabbling about them, one can almost never say. But there is no escaping the dominant *perception* achieved by politically active forces throughout Europe no later than the early eighteenth century, namely, that the antagonisms were no longer worth fighting over. A later section of this essay will examine possible explanations for the change in attitude, but at this point I should emphasize that the crucial discontinuity was the result, not of a necessary acceptance of irrefutable solutions, but rather of a willingness to stop pressing dissensions to their logical conclusion.

Although the process did not move at the same pace in every country—in England, according to J. H. Plumb, it was not consummated until the early eighteenth century, and there were certainly after-tremors in enough other countries to suggest that the transition was slow and gradual—none of the troubles of the late seventeenth century, in contrast to their predecessors, seriously threatened or fundamentally questioned the entire system of government, the very organization of politics. *That* was the crucial change, and if one has to give it a chronological dimension, one can perceive it beginning first in Germany at the end of the Thirty Years' War, and then spreading through Europe, retarded in some states by what Stephen Baxter has called the "hero kings": Louis XIV, William III, and Charles XII, dynastic monarchs having their last fling and causing a final flutter of political tension[97]—with the important difference that now the immediate source of trouble was the ruler, not the ruled, and that Europe's stability survived this challenge as easily as it passed other tests around 1700 (such as the Glorious Revolution in England or the death of William III in the Netherlands). This outcome, moreover, represented the conclusive establishment of the structure that is recognizable as the modern state, organized around an impersonal, centralized, and unifying system of government, resting on law, bureaucracy, and force. Since the mid-seventeenth-century upheavals proved to be the last major effort to resist the consolidation of that structure and to defend local autonomies, their failure marked a decisive change of direction in

97. Plumb, *Political Stability;* I am most grateful to Stephen Baxter for his personal communication on this subject in January 1973. The effects of the prince's growing powers, and the accompanying impersonalization of the state, is the theme of an excellent and all-too-brief book that reached me when this study was already in press: J. H. Shennan, *The Origins of the Modern European State 1450-1725* (London, 1974). Concentrating on domestic political relations, he perceives, despite considerable variations among the states, "a general European crisis, brought about . . . by the inflated authority of the prince against which these groups [the holders of power] reacted" (p. 112). Shennan's interpretation, though different in some of its emphases, complements in much fuller detail the argument of the present section.

the development of Western society. In this regard the heritage of the late seventeenth century has survived even the great revolutions of the eighteenth, nineteenth, and twentieth centuries.

And this quieting down after a hundred and fifty years of contest manifests itself just as clearly in the enterprise that was a barometer of political change: political thought. Throughout the sixteenth century and up to the mid-seventeenth century, political theorists were divided into irreconcilable antagonisms unlike any that one finds until the late eighteenth century, and possibly not until the rise of Marxism. There were the Machiavellians versus the anti-Machiavellians, the ideological subversives (both Huguenot and Jesuit) versus the *politiques*, constitutionalism versus the divine right of kings, and primitive egalitarianism versus absolutism. Again, the arguments did not seem to die down until the late seventeenth century, when Locke clearly bested Filmer, when Machiavelli's qualities (as opposed to his bad name) became an accepted part of political thought,[98] and when, next to a Hobbes or a Pufendorf, Bossuet sounded like a swan song. The dialectic came to an end: theses and antitheses produced syntheses, and the conflicts did not resume—certainly not at the same pitch—until the age of Burke.

98. Felix Raab, *The English Face of Machiavelli: A Changing Interpretation 1500-1700* (London, 1964).

VIII

INTERNATIONAL RELATIONS AND
THE FORCE OF RELIGION

We can trace the same succession of changes both in international relations and in the related arena of religious allegiance. Twenty years ago Garrett Mattingly demonstrated conclusively the process whereby the techniques of modern diplomacy grew, from their first significant appearance during the Italian wars, into the complex system of functions, privileges, and procedures of the age of Gondomar. A new instrument of control was thus assembled, but despite its wide use its concrete impact on events remains unclear. Some particularly talented individual ambassadors, such as Mendoza in the 1580's or Gondomar in the 1610's, could influence a country's policies, but the self-important rulers and ministers of the age rarely allowed their servants sufficient initiative to impinge upon their decisions. When Philip II, prodded by the Archdukes in the Low Countries, at last recognized the futility of his campaign against Henry IV in France and decided to make peace, he asked the Pope to arbitrate, and had his representatives reach an agreement in a mere three weeks of discussion at Vervins in 1598. No part of the negotiations suggests they were seriously affected or guided by the requirements of a new diplomacy. The implement lay at hand, but often it was little more than window-dressing—used for information gathering and not much else. As yet there did not seem to be a pressing cause to which its elaborate qualities could make a vital contribution.[99]

The need finally arose, as did so much between the mid-sixteenth

99. Garrett Mattingly, *Renaissance Diplomacy* (London, 1955); De Lamar Jensen, *Diplomacy and Dogmatism: Bernardino de Mendoza and the French Catholic League* (Cambridge, Mass., 1964): A. E. Imhof, *Der Friede von Vervins 1598* (Aarau, 1966).

and the mid-seventeenth century, because of the consequences of war. For as soon as new dimensions of destruction became available, they were pursued. On the one hand princes could crush their great nobles' capacity for resistance, cannonading into obsolescence the previous inviolability of a formidable castle. On the other hand they could look with new eyes on their neighbors. In an age of ideological fervor, old-fashioned claims to lands and thrones took on a bitterness that led to ever more devastating aggressions.

Charles V may have believed in it for a while, but the ideal of a universal Christian empire had lost its meaning by the time he abdicated in the 1550's. By then religious compulsions were exacerbating rather than moderating political ambitions and divisions. And so, with nothing but financial limitations to hold them back. Europe's monarchs could give free rein to increasingly destructive ambitions. The Italian states had led the way in the fifteenth century, but after 1494 they gradually came to be joined by the rest of the Continent. Already those acute observers, Commines, Machiavelli, and Guicciardini, were describing a new cynicism in foreign affairs, and when, by the mid-sixteenth century, the combatants had exhausted their possibilities in Italy, a wider battleground beckoned. Charles V had at different times been engaged in hostilities as far apart as Vienna, Mühlberg, and Tunis; but this was as nothing compared with the *simultaneous* hostilities his son sustained. Philip II's soldiers in the 1570's roamed the eastern Mediterranean, the Caribbean, and the Netherlands. By the end of the reign they were to add Ireland and France to their range of operations. As the fighting became endemic almost throughout the Continent, "improved" constantly by innovative technology, an incipient anarchy began to hover over international affairs. Even the seeming exceptions partook of the mounting callousness. Although England might appear to have been less involved than most countries, her atrocities in Ireland and the tactics of the "sea dogs" at a time of undeclared war hardly indicated a different pattern of behavior. Mattingly had no doubt about the result. The progress toward regularity of forms, in which "European states . . . [could] live together in one system," was crushingly interrupted. "The clash of ideological absolutes," he concluded, "drives diplomacy from the field."[100]

100. *Renaissance Diplomacy*, pp. 195 and 196.

The nadir of helplessness was reached in the Thirty Years' War. Neither in scale nor in brutality, neither in geographic reach nor in indiscriminacy yet ferocity of partisanship, had armies behaved in this fashion before. The minimum of one-third of the population of central Europe that died as a direct or indirect result of the war stands as mute testimony to its unparalleled devastation.[101] Wallenstein's "living off the land" and Gustavus Adolphus' "swath of destruction" were tactics whose far-reaching viciousness had never been equaled in a thousand years of Western history. Michael Roberts' summing up reveals both the new geographic spread and the multiplication of troops that changed the face of war:

> [In] the Thirty Years' War . . . battle came again into favour [after the sterility of much of the fighting around 1600]. . . . As hostilities ranged back and forth over Germany, and along the borders of Germany . . . , commanders were driven to look at the whole of central Europe as one great theatre of war. When Gustav Adolf wrote that "all the wars of Europe are now blended into one," he was thinking in terms of politics; but the remark was equally true in regard to strategy. Wallenstein sends Arnim to fight on the Vistula; Pappenheim rushes to the relief of Maestricht; Olivares dreams of seizing Göteborg . . . ; Savoy, Venice, Transylvania and even the Tatars of the Crimea become elements in ever-wider and more unified plans of operations. . . . Gustav Adolf's strategic thinking . . . [was] more complex, vaster, than any one commander had ever previously attempted. . . . [After his death] the strategy of devastation began to be employed with a new thoroughness and logic. . . . [The result was] the great increase in the scope of warfare, reflected in a corresponding increase in the normal size of . . . armies. . . . The previous millennium could show nothing to compare with this sudden rise in the size of western European armies. Great agglomerations of troops for a particular occasion had indeed occurred in the past . . . but in the West, at least, the seventeenth century saw the permanent establishment of some armies at levels which earlier ages had rarely, if ever, known. . . . That Gustav Adolf had 175,000 men under arms in 1632 was for Sweden a quite exceptional circumstance,

101. See my "The Effects of the Thirty Years' War on the German Economy," *The Journal of Modern History*, XXXIV (1962), 40-51, and the literature cited there.

never repeated. But this does not alter the fact that the scale of European warfare was throughout the century prodigiously increasing: the great armies of Louis XIV [reaching 400,000] had to be met by armies of comparable size.[102]

This process made its first major leap forward during the Thirty Years' War, and when one recalls that for every soldier there were something like five camp followers,[103] one quickly understands the immensity of the impact made by decades of almost ceaseless and merciless warfare.

The appalled reaction of those who watched Europe literally tearing itself apart was to be a fundamental cause of the change in perceptions that produced the post-"crisis" resolution. That will be discussed below, as part of an effort to explain why the resolution occurred. But it is important to point out here that, as in other areas of activity, in international relations the chaos inspired attempts at control as well as dismay. The first great milestone in the modern study of international law was raised by Hugo Grotius, whose pioneering *The Law of War and Peace* was published in 1625. Seeking to fashion a new and acceptable structure that could govern the relations among states, he gave a powerful impetus to the thesis that he elaborated so forcefully in his book—that there *are* laws of war and peace, even in a Europe of independent, sovereign, and secular governments, none of which acknowledges any restraints on its actions. Grotius thus provided the theoretical underpinnings for a renewal of the belief that a settled framework for international relations could be achieved.

To create such a framework, however, a totally new mechanism was necessary, more effective than the shifting networks of alliances so common during the war.[104] And therein lay the importance

102. *Essays in Swedish History*, pp. 202-4.
103. C. V. Wedgwood, *The Thirty Years War* (London, 1938)—the discussion of camp followers is on p. 376 of the Garden City, 1961 edition.
104. The ideological blocs of the Thirty Years' War—one Catholic, centered in Brussels, the other Protestant, centered in Amsterdam—are examined in: F. H. Schubert, *Ludwig Camerarius (1573-1651). Eine Biographie* (Kallmünz, 1955); Dieter Albrecht, *Die Auswärtige Politik Maximilians von Bayern, 1618-1635* (Göttingen, 1962); and Georg Lutz, *Kardinal Giovanni Francesco Guidi di Bagno: Politik und Religion im Zeitalter Richelieus und Urbans VIII* (Tübingen, 1971).

of Westphalia—as much for what it started as for what it ended. Breaking with precedent completely, this peace was not simply an *ad hoc* agreement between two or three enemies, settling a few disputed issues. Rather, it was conceived of as the answer to anarchy: a once-and-for-ever settlement, agreed to by *all* the major powers, of *all* the outstanding problems of western and central Europe. The range of the decisions, symbolized by the recognition of the independence of two new states, the United Provinces and the Swiss Confederation, stands in startling contrast to previous treaties like Cateau-Cambrésis or Vervins, which involved only two or three states and were concerned mainly with border areas. Now the whole map of Europe was being drawn for future reference. It is no wonder that the treaties took seven years to negotiate, or that in the process diplomacy should have come to occupy the central, formalized place in governmental activities that Richelieu had foreseen.[105] Some important matters were left in abeyance despite the seven-year ordeal, but within twelve years the treaties of the Pyrenees, Copenhagen, and Oliva were regarded as having completed and rounded out the edifice that had been created in outline at Westphalia. And all of Louis XIV's wars and peace agreements were similarly viewed as variations on a theme set in 1648. They were adjustments to a system whose essential structure remained unaltered because, despite loose ends, men presumed that the map of Europe had been drawn for eternity.

Wars and maneuverings continued, of course, but they were now understood within the context of an ordered diplomatic system, whose conventions and assumptions were universally accepted, and not as omens of unbridled chaos. Remarkably enough, the next major international peace congress, at Utrecht in 1713, was still perceived as an attempt to realign the framework that had been established at Westphalia and had not essentially been altered, despite decades of fighting and negotiation.[106] That this institution, the all-

105. Richelieu, *Testament politique*, ed. Louis André (Paris, 1947), pp. 347 ff. Fritz Dickmann, *Der westfälische Frieden* (Münster, 1959). Substantively, of course, the treaty also initiated one very important shift: from Spain to France as the dominant force in international relations after 150 years of conflict.
106. Ogg, *Europe in the Seventeenth Century*, 8th edition (New York,

in-one treaty, survived down to the twentieth century—renewing itself with monotonous regularity at Utrecht, Paris, Versailles I and Versailles II, until the procedure finally lost its force—is the best testimony to its impact on the European consciousness as a remedy for irrepressible and accelerating instability and disorder.

The critical element in the change was not some definable objective circumstance, but the *perception* of the classes active in politics. What mattered was that after Westphalia their perspective changed. Long-standing problems were not really solved forever (with the one exception that, as we shall see, religion did cease to affect foreign policies), but the elite stopped assuming that the problems were insoluble. The image may have been more impressive than the reality, but leading Europeans did now believe that they were working within a system, whereas from the Italian Wars to the Thirty Years' War no such belief had seemed possible.

John Locke's reaction to the Restoration, written a few months after Charles II's return to England, was symptomatic of this newly found attachment to stability, however tenuously and perhaps even self-deludingly the tranquility had been achieved:

> I no sooner perceived myself in the world but I found myself in a storm, which hath lasted almost hitherto, and therefore cannot but entertain the approaches of a calm with the greatest joy and satisfaction; and this methinks obliges me, both in duty and gratitude, to be chary of such a blessing, and what lies in me to endeavour its continuance, by disposing men's minds to obedience to that government which brought with it that quiet and settlement which our own giddy folly had put beyond the reach, not only of our contrivance, but hopes.[107]

1962), p. 179; Clark, *The Seventeenth Century*, 2nd edition (Oxford, 1947), p. 135.

107. John Locke, *Two Tracts on Government*, ed. Philip Abrams (Cambridge, 1967), pp. 119-20. Obviously, it is impossible to make a case for general perceptions, even among the elite, from the comments, however sensitive, of one observer. The basic problem in an essay of this size is the impossibility of building up a sufficient number of quotations to enhance the plausibility of the argument. When discussing the perceptions of the elite, the historian is relying on his own quite fallible impressions anyhow. I make no claim for unanimity, of course—merely

If so limited an event as Charles II's restoration could foster the feelings of relief expressed in that sentence, one can imagine the emotion, the expectation of eternal bliss, that sustained the burghers of Olmütz as they thanked God, not for ending thirty years of war, but for ensuring that it would not recur: "Thou hast set a bound that they [the soldiers] may not pass over; that they turn not again to cover the earth."[108] People felt that a decisive corner had been turned, whether in fact it had been or not, and their *conviction* of change was the vital element in the mid-century transformation of international affairs.

*   *   *

Essential to this progression, and a corollary to it, was the decline of religion as a stimulus to violence. Whatever one estimates the level of personal or public commitment to religious belief to have been in the fifteenth century, the cataclysmic rise of fervor after Luther's questioning of the sale of indulgences in 1517 is inescapable. And the consistency of the influence of dogma on events was unvarying for more than a hundred years. But by the middle of the seventeenth century its impact on politics (if not on private beliefs) was dwindling rapidly. Until the 1630's and 1640's, the outcome of the struggles over faith remained in doubt, and no government could ignore the force of the passions they aroused. Thereafter, however, religion ceased to be a violent issue. Fewer and fewer men died for their beliefs, a phenomenon not unrelated to the decline in witchcraft executions.

This calming began in international relations. Whereas both Protestant and Catholic networks of alliances transcended national interests during at least the first half of the Thirty Years' War,[109] they had vanished by the 1650's. When Gustavus Adolphus was

---

for what I sense to have been predominant attitudes, primarily among the literate and active classes. The equally difficult problem of explaining changes in perception, which would require intensive study of media of communication, letters, and the nature of mass psychology, must also lie beyond the scope of this essay. I would like to thank William Beik for his invaluable remarks on these issues.

108. Quoted by Wedgwood, *Thirty Years War*, p. 485.
109. See above, note 104.

saving German Protestantism in 1631, the support he received from Catholic France seemed scandalous, and before sending subsidies to the Swedish king, Cardinal Richelieu looked anxiously toward Rome (where, however, a papacy of reviving worldliness under Urban VIII found its own reasons to prefer anti-Hapsburg to pro-Catholic policies).[110] Just twenty years later the remorseless enemy of Catholicism, Oliver Cromwell, considered alliances with Spain and France before signing a treaty of friendship with Cardinal Mazarin, fought a war against his co-religionists, the Dutch, and, most important, aroused little surprise by his actions. Thereafter one's church was to all intents and purposes irrelevant to one's foreign policy. When Pope Innocent X, more staunch than his predecessor as an upholder of the faith, denounced the Peace of Westphalia as "null, void, invalid, iniquitous, unjust, damnable, reprobate, inane, empty of meaning and effect for all time," he was politely ignored[111]—the fate of the papacy, and thus of religion in politics, henceforth.

If toleration came more slowly within individual states, that might only have been expected, given the *cuius regio* mentality of the time. Yet some contemporaries were apparently fooled by developments in international affairs, and expected a similar relaxation on the home front before it actually arrived. The time lag was especially traumatic for the Huguenots, who, like most Europeans, were caught

110. See Lutz, *Bagno*, pp. 394 ff., 474 ff., 508, and 514 ff.; A. Leman, *Urbain VIII et la rivalité de la France et de la maison d'Autriche de 1631 à 1635* (Lille, 1920). A significant contrast is provided by, on the one hand, Richelieu insisting that Gustavus guarantee not to molest the Catholic religion; and, on the other hand, Urban VIII ingenuously telling the Emperor Ferdinand II that the war in Germany was not a war of religion.

111. Wedgwood, *Thirty Years War*, p. 506. In England, a non-participating country, the impression had already taken hold by the 1630's that the war was no longer a religious conflict: Walter H. Schumacher, *Vox Populi: The Thirty Years' War in English Newspapers and Pamphlets* (unpub. Ph.D. diss., Princeton, 1975), chapter 6. The best recent discussion of the more general issue of religion's waning influence is William J. Bouwsma, "The Secularization of Society in the Seventeenth Century," *XIII International Congress of Historical Sciences* (Moscow, 1970). Bouwsma relates his theme in passing (p. 14) to the "general crisis" thesis.

totally unawares by the Revocation of the Edict of Nantes.[112] Nevertheless, it is probably fair to say that this last flurry of intolerance (which included repressions in the Netherlands and England, notably the Clarendon Code) owed at least as much to political as to religious motivations. And after the 1660's killing in the name of faith was virtually unknown, as fanaticism and millenarianism died away, and the great churches, Calvinist as well as Catholic, which had seemed so vital and lively only a few years before, lost their ability to produce heroes or saints. Whether personified by Bossuet or symbolized by the attack on Bayle, orthodoxy everywhere was on the defensive. An issue of endless ramifications, the source of perennial discord, had at last been brought under control. If the mid-century resolution had consisted of no more than this, it would have deserved close attention as a critical moment in European history.

112. See my "St. Bartholomew and Historical Perspective," *The Massacre of Saint Bartholomew: Reappraisals and Documents,* ed. A. Soman (The Hague, 1974), pp. 252-55. A major reason that the Huguenots were fooled was the decline of fervor after the 1650's among Frenchmen, who have been described felicitously as "A Generation of Tartuffes" in Orest Ranum, *Paris in the Age of Absolutism: An Essay* (New York, 1968), chapter 11. I should mention that the process being described here was only *within* Christianity; the struggle against Islam continued long after Protestant versus Catholic conflict had subsided.

IX

ECONOMICS, DEMOGRAPHY,
AND SOCIAL RELATIONS

The last major category to be considered—economic, demographic, and social change—brings us to the area in which Hobsbawm first posited the "crisis." Ironically, however, it is the one aspect of sixteenth- and seventeenth-century history in which the progression noticeable elsewhere becomes unclear and imprecise. The contradictions and the absence of a crisp pattern have inspired the main criticisms of Hobsbawm's formulation; these criticisms have in turn aroused most of the basic doubts about the entire "crisis" thesis; and thus, paradoxically, the very field in which the interpretation originated has promoted the uneasiness and confusion that still becloud the meaning, validity, and applicability of the "crisis." The lack of neat economic or demographic shifts has provided fuel for doubt from the start—the worry is common to such different evaluators as Stone, Lublinskaya, and Goubert—and it is time to admit that the larger case cannot rest on evidence from this quarter. However conclusive the studies completed by the early 1950's might have seemed to Hobsbawm, their unambiguous implications have now been blurred.[113] Consequently, although the inspiration for the "crisis" literature came from economics and demography, those fields can no longer offer the basis or even the starting-point for the argument. But that is not to say that they must be abandoned. The relationship is still there, albeit more subtle and indirect than was once thought.

To be sure, no great amount of digging into monographic studies is required to reveal that the chronology of economic and demographic change in this period is in some disarray. One recent general

113. See the works cited in notes 2 and 5 of Hobsbawm's article in *Crisis in Europe*.

survey speaks of "the European crisis of 1600-1740." Other historians, on the contrary, prefer to think in terms of recurrent, severe, but essentially short-term conjunctions of famine, plague, and the collapse of the means of subsistence: brief and localized "crises of subsistence." The most detailed study of general trends perceives a major turndown beginning in 1619, while some French scholarship suggests that the indicators of growth and well-being reveal no pattern at all, especially when investigated at the local level, or at most a general decline beginning around 1680. For the Dutch and Swedes, of course, the decades that supposedly witnessed the worst depression and population stagnation prove to have been their most prosperous and expansive period.[114]

The prime difficulty is the persistence of the locality or the region as a relatively autonomous and self-sufficient economic unit. Outside interference did grow, especially in the form of efforts to distribute food according to need, but the resistance to the forces of centralization tended to be much more successful in economics than in politics, primarily because the former was still so poorly understood, even by such arch-interventionists as Colbert. In this respect, Europe had changed only in minor ways between 1500 and 1700 (a serious difficulty for Hobsbawm's thesis). Consequently, throughout the seventeenth century the incidence of growth, both

114. M. Reinhard, A. Armengaud, and J. Dupaquier, *Histoire générale de la population mondiale* (Paris, 1968), chapter X: "La Crise européenne de 1600 à 1740." The first discussion of the "subsistence crisis" was Jean Meuvret's "Les Crises de subsistances et de la démographie de la France de l'ancien régime," *Population*, I (1946), 543-50. For more recent work, see Pierre Goubert, "Historical Demography and the Reinterpretation of Early Modern French History: A Research Review," *Journal of Interdisciplinary History*, I (1970), 37-48. The general economic reversal of 1619 has been elaborated by Romano in "Tra XVI e XVII Secolo," and "Encore la crise de 1619-1622," *Annales*, XIX (1964), 31-37. See, too, Pierre Chaunu, "Le Renversement de la tendance majeure des prix et des activités au XVIIe siècle: problèmes de fait et de methode," *Studi in Onore di Amintore Fanfani*, IV (Milan, 1962), pp. 219-55. The indeterminate conclusions of local studies are surveyed in Goubert, "Local History," an analysis that is reinforced by Paul G. Spagnoli, "Demographic History from Parish Monographs: The Problem of Local Variations," *Journal of Interdisciplinary History* (forthcoming), which also cites the most recent literature.

in wealth and in population, often remained haphazard, dependent on the sometimes accidental answers to vital questions: How far will a plague reach? Where has the weather ruined a harvest? Is warfare close at hand?[115]

Yet there is no denying that, in contrast to both the sixteenth and the eighteenth centuries, just about every locality in Europe suffered a major setback, with serious consequences, at some time during the seventeenth century. In some areas the downturn began as early as 1600 (the so-called "great Atlantic" or "Cantabrian" plague that struck down half a million victims in Spain between 1597 and 1602, with an echo of 30,000 deaths in London in 1603); in others as late as the 1680's (Provence, for example, feeling no ill effects until the Franco-Dutch war). But virtually no region escaped totally the experience of devastating misfortune, whether through plague, famine, war, or depression. Although local resources and conditions—and plain good luck—could ameliorate some of the impact, there were enough all-encompassing forces for ill to ensure hardship for everyone. The economic depression that struck northern Europe and England in the 1620's was felt throughout those countries, as were the effects of the debasements that were one of its principal causes; there was similar uniformity to the terrible plague and prolonged subsistence crisis that hit the Mediterranean area around 1630 (sweeping away perhaps half the population of Lyons and something like one million inhabitants of northern Italy), and to its even wider ranging successor of the mid-1650's to mid-1660's, which killed more than 100,000 people in Naples in 1656 and in London in 1665, and over a fifth of the population of Denmark in the 1650's; while the "little ice age" that began in the late sixteenth century,

---

115. The clearest exposition of the link between the appearance of economic difficulties in a locality and a demographic crisis is in Goubert's monumental study, *Cent Mille Provinciaux*, pp. 68-82 and 99-101 (full citation in the Bibliographic Appendix, II). For the connection between a decline and the experience of war, see Henry Kamen, "The Social and Economic Consequences of the Thirty Years' War," *Past & Present*, No. 39 (1968), 44-61. Another perspective is offered by Hermann Rebel, "Probleme der oberösterreichischen Sozialgeschichte zur Zeit der bayerischen Pfandherrschaft, 1620-1628," *Jahrbuch des oberösterreichischen Musealvereines*, 115 (1970), 155-65.

with its acute stage of cold vegetative periods between 1617 and 1650, and its decade of striking glacial advance from 1643 to 1653, knew no boundaries.[116] If to these broad agencies of deterioration one adds the consequences of war (especially the Thirty Years' War), of soaring taxation, and of revolt and upheaval at mid-century, one must conclude that those few regions whose prosperity was uninterrupted until the last third of the century were decided exceptions. Even some vital indicators of the well-being of the Dutch, those exemplars of wealth who were in the midst of their Golden Age, show significant reversals at mid-century: land reclamation slowed down dramatically in the 1640's, as did most of the indices of prices and population.[117]

It would seem fair to say, therefore, that at the local level the cyclical difficulties of the sixteenth century, interspersed within an enormous boom, were replaced in the seventeenth century by a real break in economic and demographic advance. At best, these hundred years can be seen as a time of stagnation, the antecedent to renewed advance on all fronts in the eighteenth century. But this is no more than a very rough and blunt impression; and the piling up of local studies may not heighten precision significantly. One sim-

116. For some basic recent works on local history, plague, and demographic and economic trends, see the Bibliographic Appendix, III. On climate, see G. Utterström, "Climatic Fluctuations and Population Problems in Early Modern History," *Scandinavian Economic History Review*, III (1955), 3-47; Emmanuel Le Roy Ladurie, *Times of Feast, Times of Famine: A History of Climate since the Year 1000* (Garden City, 1971: a revised translation of the original French version published in 1967); the long review of Le Roy Ladurie by John D. Post: "Meteorological Historiography," *Journal of Interdisciplinary History*, III (1973), 721-32; Braudel, *La Méditerranée*, Part I, chapter IV; and Anne-Marie Piuz, "Climat, récoltes et vie des hommes à Genève, XVIe-XVIIIe siècle," *Annales*, XXIX (1974), 599-618.

117. Jan de Vries, *The Dutch Rural Economy in the Golden Age, 1500-1700* (New Haven, 1974), p. 194 and the graphs on pp. 89-95 and 176-80. For a brilliant evocation of the other end of the spectrum, the relentless decline of the great Italian cities, see Eric Cochrane, *Florence in the Forgotten Centuries, 1527-1800: A History of Florence and the Florentines in the Age of the Grand Dukes* (Chicago, 1973), especially the section on Galileo, which links the economic difficulties of 1620-50 quite directly with cultural change.

ply has to admit that regional variation was enormous, and that sharp patterns and well-defined waves of movement are unlikely to crystallize in the quicksilver experiences of Europe's localities.

Nevertheless, on the larger canvas the changes are unmistakable. The influx of precious metals slumped precipitously, and many decades passed before they were replaced by the new sources of overseas wealth, such as tobacco and sugar. The yield of crops dropped in the seventeenth century for the first time since the late middle ages. Another basic index of prosperity, the Sound dues, reached a peak between 1580 and 1620, and then declined; to which the most wide-ranging of recent studies of general economic trends has added an even more dismal catalogue: all indices, whether of prices, industrial and agricultural production, or trade, reveal a transition from boom to stagnation following the well-nigh universal economic crisis around 1619-22. At the same time the flight to the cities, with their dreadful mortality; the hardships of vagrancy; and the steady emigration overseas; all accentuated the slackening of population growth at the aggregate level. Continent-wide, Europe's inhabitants probably doubled in the course of the sixteenth century, but at best increased by about one-third in the succeeding hundred years. The signs of hard times are inescapable.[118]

Whether this evidence substantiates Hobsbawm's view that the changes between 1600 and 1700 amounted to a "fundamental . . .

118. Hamilton, *American Treasure*, p. 34; in a forthcoming book, Kenneth Maxwell demonstrates that the precious metals were being mined in the same quantities, but remained in the New World in the seventeenth century. The shift in the center of gravity and vitality in the Spanish empire from Iberia to the New World is a theme of the second volume of Lynch, *Spain under the Habsburgs*. Indispensable is H. and P. Chaunu, *Séville et l'Atlantique (1504-1650)* (Paris, 1955-59). See further note 120, below. On agriculture: B. H. Slicher van Bath, *The Agrarian History of Western Europe, A.D. 500-1850* (London, 1963) and *Yield Ratios, 810-1820* (Wageningen, 1963). On other economic indicators: N. E. Bang, *Tabeller over Skibsfart og Varetransport gennen Øresund 1497-1660* (Copenhagen, 1906-22); A. Christensen, *Dutch Trade and the Baltic about 1600* (Copenhagen, 1940); and Romano, "Tra XVI e XVII Secolo." For general population trends, the best survey is Helleiner in the *Cambridge Economic History*. On vagrancy, see A. L. Beier, "Vagrants and the Social Order in Elizabethan England," *Past & Present*, No. 64 (1974), 3-29.

solution of the difficulties which had previously stood in the way of the triumph of capitalism" is a different matter, however. There is little to show that Europe's institutions benefited significantly from the cold shower they had undergone—that wealth was more productively used and in more effective hands by 1700 than it had been in 1600. There was somewhat more capital accumulation, especially in joint-stock companies and in the public sector; there were a few new institutions, such as the public banks of Holland and England; but there was as much courtly extravagance—at Whitehall (and later Windsor) or Schönbrunn no less than at Versailles—as before; markets, agriculture, forms of expenditure, and economic roles had not been transformed; and it was by no means clear until well into the eighteenth century that overseas possessions were a prime instrument of economic advance. There has been a similar argument about the effects of the Thirty Years' War in Germany: that disaster somehow was beneficial in the long run, sweeping away inefficiency and misallocation of resources. That theory is now thoroughly discredited, and in the case of the "crisis," too, one needs documentation beyond the mere reversal itself to show how it achieved specific fruitful consequences.[119]

The two profound changes that did take place in the seventeenth century were of a different order. The first was one of the great shifts of European history: the movement of the economic, commercial, and industrial center of the Continent from the Mediterranean, where it had lain for over 2000 years, to the north and west. No such process can be regarded as sudden or unheralded, and indeed its roots lay as far back as the fifteenth century. Moreover, the main cause of the reorientation may not have been so much the depression of the period as the surprising capacity of the northerners to recover quickly, while the South lagged behind. But there can be no minimizing the importance of the few decisive decades. *Circa* 1590 the Mediterranean still led the way; by the 1650's she no longer did, not even in her own trade.[120] This was another of the

119. Hobsbawm, "Crisis," pp. 5-6. On the interpretation of the Thirty Years' War, see my *The Thirty Years' War*, 2nd edition (Lexington, Mass., 1972), esp. the article by Steinberg.

120. One of the decisive shifts, the conquest of Mediterranean trade by Dutchmen and Englishmen, is surveyed in Ralph Davis, "England and

new and permanent situations that emerged in the seventeenth century—not, in this case, the resolution of a problem, but a momentous alteration nonetheless.

The second change, possibly related to the first, and certainly an outgrowth of the rise of overseas empires, was the appearance in the mid-seventeenth century of wars motivated solely by commercial ambitions. Perhaps it was the dissipation of religious passions as a force for war that opened the way for economics; perhaps it was the growing interest in the mechanisms of economics and the resultant rise of mercantilist beliefs; or perhaps the diversification of economic activity merely provided more occasions for conflict and antagonism. Whatever the reason, the onslaught against the Dutch by the English and French from the 1650's to 1670's—a basic cause of the Republic's descent from her position of supremacy in Europe's commerce—was the first international confrontation inspired essentially by the needs of merchants and manufacturers, and conducted despite ties of religion and other interests.[121] Again, this was

---

the Mediterranean," *Essays in the Economic and Social History of Tudor and Stuart England in Honour of R. H. Tawney*, ed. F. J. Fisher (Cambridge, 1961), pp. 117-37. See, too, H. R. Trevor-Roper, "Religion, the Reformation and Social Change" in his book of the same title (London, 1967), pp. 1-45. One subject that might bear further study is the possibility that the root of the differentiation between South and North lies in the contrast between Spain's overseas empire, which diminished steadily as a source of wealth for the Mediterranean (see above, note 118) at the very time that England and the Netherlands were beginning to reap multiplying profits from their overseas interests. It is obviously time for a new assessment of this crucial problem in European history—one that would take into account recent demographic findings and would perhaps give long overdue recognition to the evaluation of the Mediterranean's decline in Richard Ehrenberg's *Das Zeitalter der Fugger* (Jena, 1896; English edition, 1928), where the different methods of public finance in North and South are shown to have had momentous consequences.

121. Charles Wilson, *Profit and Power, a Study of England and the Dutch Wars* (London, 1957); J. E. Farnell, "The Navigation Act of 1651, the First Dutch War and the London Merchant Community," *Economic History Review*, 2nd series, XVI (1964), 439-54; L. A. Harper, *The English Navigation Laws: A Seventeenth-Century Experience in Social Engineering* (New York, 1939). With the precedent established, of

in no way a "resolution," but by the same token it cannot be seen as part of a "crisis" in Hobsbawm's terms, except in so far as it reveals the growing saliency of economic concerns.

Thus the progression of events in economic and demographic history cannot be made to conform to the stages that have been perceived in other aspects of seventeenth-century developments. It was an uneasy, cautious time, preceded and followed by periods of advance which were in no way dependent on the hiatus that separated them. And the important changes that did take place do not fit convincingly into any of the broader frameworks of "crisis" that have been imposed on the period. They certainly fail to provide the foundation for such an interpretation.

*   *   *

If we shift our sights somewhat, however, interesting connections begin to emerge. As has already been stressed, it is the impact of a situation—its image—rather than its exact reality, that often allows us most clearly to understand the changes that were overtaking European society. And this is as true in economics and demography as it is in politics and religion. By concentrating on the *effects* of the boom and subsequent stagnation, rather than on the events themselves, we can expose the links with the other changes of the time.

Seen in these terms, the advances of the sixteenth century were similar to the uncertainties of the seventeenth in that both seemed to be bewildering innovations totally beyond the power of man to control. Whether ostensibly beneficial or harmful, their effects were equally volatile—not only in stimulating social change but also in contributing to the sense of dislocation caused by the crumbling of familiar landmarks. The effects of both situations were thus parallel, except that, as Trevor-Roper has suggested, the growth after 1500 may have provided a release of tensions which then vanished during the contraction after 1600 and thus allowed political unrest to reach the boiling point.[122] About the basic effects, however, there

---

course, commercial antagonisms loomed large in almost every war thereafter: the Spanish Succession, for instance, would probably have been decided peacefully had Louis not tried to subvert English and Dutch overseas trade.

122. Trevor-Roper, "General Crisis," pp. 79-80.

can be no doubt. First, in the sixteenth century, the causes of disruption pressed in from all sides: the meteoric and relentless inflation, unlike any that Europe had ever experienced; the discovery of strange new people and places overseas, blessed with undreamed of riches; the intensifying sense of overpopulation, as vagabondage and banditry became ever more pressing concerns; the sudden fortunes and equally sudden disasters as the rising demand for food and goods enriched some but destroyed others; and the social mobility made possible by new accumulations of wealth. These and related influences conspired to undermine many of the most familiar social and economic relationships.

Nor did the subsequent reversal of some of these trends bring about any relief. Rather, they merely confirmed for the victims of social and economic forces that stability, certainty, and predictability had in effect become unattainable. It was disturbing, for instance, that new classes had risen to prominence—the English gentry, the French *noblesse de robe*—while others had lost status—the German knights, the English peerage, the Spanish *picaros*. At the same time, confronted by financial difficulties, landowners were raising rents alarmingly, thus inhibiting further gains by the lower orders, and the newly risen social classes were trying to slam the door of mobility shut behind them.[123] The end of the boom thus removed the flexibility that had arisen during the sixteenth century, both in financial investment and in social relations. What was noticeable in particular was that the previously new situation, to which Europeans might at least have grown accustomed, was now

123. For the literature on classes, mobility, and rents, see the Bibliographic Appendix, IV. The epitome of the closing off of mobility was the institution of the *paulette* in France. The gradually changing impact of the sale of office has been superbly analyzed in Roland Mousnier, *La Vénalité des offices sous Henri IV et Louis XIII* (Rouen, 1945). See, too, J. H. Shennan, *The Parlement of Paris* (London, 1968), pp. 114 ff., and the excellent general discussion in Kamen, *Iron Century*, esp. Part II: "Society." On another aspect of the seigneurial reaction, the nobility's tightening grip on the land, see H. J. Habakkuk, "Marriage Settlements in the Eighteenth Century," *Transactions of the Royal Historical Society*, 4th series, 32 (1950), 15-30. The equivalent process among city patriciates is traced by Peter Burke, *Venice & Amsterdam: A Study of Seventeenth-Century Elites* (London, 1974).

rendered obsolete in turn. Change was the order of the day; none of the old (or even the new) guideposts remained reliable for long.

In other words, the economic and demographic change of the period fits our outline inasmuch as it contributed to the sense of disorder and helplessness characteristic of the first stage, the dislocation, that was described earlier in this essay. It is in the realm of perception that the model dovetails. By the same token, we also find the movement toward settlement taking place—albeit less distinctly—as the period closes. This progression was associated with the one decisive reaction that did arise in response to economic and demographic developments: government intervention. The institutions and structures that were altered to meet the new challenges were not those in the economic sphere, as Hobsbawm suggests, but in the political sphere. The main concern was to find some means of controlling, not so much the forces themselves, but their effects. Governments had to deal with the beggar and the vagabond on an unprecedented scale; they also had to consider problems of local disorders and regulate both the economy and food supply more extensively than ever before. Out of such needs grew the first advocacies of mercantilist policies, together with a host of new administrative activities in the realm of social welfare. These in turn were a major stimulus to the growth of governments, and hence to the crystallization of other aspects of the mid-seventeenth-century "crisis." By the end of the century, however, the bureaucracy's new role had been almost universally accepted. City fathers, merchants, professionals, and paupers alike looked to the government to mitigate the effects of economic and social change.[124] And that predilection—the hope for salvation from the center—has remained a part of Western civilization ever since.

124. The literature on mercantilism is comprehensively surveyed in Minchinton, *Mercantilism.* An example of the government's new activism, its efforts in food distribution, is admirably treated in Louise Tilly, "The Food Riot as a Form of Political Conflict in France," *Journal of Interdisciplinary History,* II (1971), 23-57. See, too, Vincent Ponko, Jr., *The Privy Council and the Spirit of Elizabethan Economic Management,* 1558-1603 (Philadelphia, 1968); E. M. Leonard, *The Early History of English Poor Relief* (Cambridge, 1900); and note 130, below. In Steensgaard's terms, this increased intervention represented a shift of economic power and capital accumulation to the public sector.

At the village level another transition of no less import was taking place. Recent research has left little doubt that the first great assault on traditional community life in the West took place in the wake of the many new developments that were set in motion around 1500.[125] The end of the scarcity of labor; the new profits available to agricultural producers; the Reformation and then the Counter-Reformation, both of which deliberately penetrated to the most remote settlements in a way no previous religious movements had; the opportunities that opened up with migration, and the population pressures that encouraged geographic mobility; the impingement of representatives of the central government on previously tightly self-contained regions; and the gradual distancing that took place between great lords and the social inferiors they dominated; all conspired to break up the ties that for centuries had distinguished the small clusters of habitations that contained most of the peoples of Europe.

Thus the new availability of labor, together with the rising profits of food producers, widened the economic cleavages among neighbors. The appearance of well-trained and educated priests and ministers, who were bent upon destroying vestigial paganism, and who imposed external, uniform standards of belief, weakened one of the essential bonds that had held isolated districts together—their common cultural assumptions. As those who fared poorly in the new situation headed for urban areas, lured by vague notions of better opportunities in towns, the familiar composition of a village's in-

---

125. See above, pp. 35-36. Although research on the history of the family is still too preliminary to justify incorporation into the catalogue that follows, one cannot avoid the significance of the conclusion reached by the pioneer in the field—that the seventeenth century was decisive for the emergence of a new status for children, and a new tenderness among close kin, because the community was losing its socializing function and the family was taking its place: Philippe Ariès, *Centuries of Childhood: A Social History of Family Life*, trans. Robert Baldick (New York, 1962), pp. 46-49 and 346-53. I can but add that changes in organization and self-perception not only reflected, but were the inevitable consequence of, the reorientations described in the next few paragraphs. For more recent work, and extensive citations of the current literature, see the two issues devoted to the history of the family by *The Journal of Interdisciplinary History*, II, No. 2 (1971), and V, No. 4 (1975).

habitants began to change. At the same time, those who remained began to encounter new forces in the shape of bureaucrats who were arriving to do the government's business throughout the realm —impose justice, raise taxes, and administer all kinds of regulations, from food distribution to poor relief. By contrast, the traditional authority, the local lord, was slowly withdrawing from his ancient role as the arbiter of village affairs, turning his attention increasingly to the rewards of Court life and office, and the joys of a social "season" and a town house. This trend was the obverse of the domestication of the nobility, and its consequences were as important for the locality as for the structure of politics.[126]

Scholarship has only just started to unveil the consequences of these disruptions among western Europe's peasantry. It is plain, however, that the villagers grew much more vulnerable to disturbance and aggressive behavior. They were ready for the hostility aroused by economic change, by widening social cleavages, and by both Reformation and Counter-Reformation. The result was that,

126. John Bossy, "The Counter-Reformation and the People of Catholic Europe," *Past & Present*, No. 47 (1970), 51-70; Michael Walzer, *The Revolution of the Saints: A Study in the Origins of Radical Politics* (Cambridge, Mass., 1965); Thomas, *Magic*, esp. chapters 2-6 and 21-22; Tilly, "Food Riot"; note 123, above; and, for a magisterial survey of the organization of peasant life, including the citation of the main literature, Jerome Blum, "The Internal Structure and Polity of the European Village Community from the Fifteenth to the Nineteenth Century," *The Journal of Modern History*, 43 (1971), 541-76. Blum sees the real disintegration of village life occurring during the eighteenth century, but many of the forces he regards as responsible—increasing seigneurial exploitation, intervention by the central government, and growing stratification and poverty—he traces back to the sixteenth century: see esp. pp. 566, 568-69, and 571-72. In a companion article, Blum has traced the emergence of the villages' community structure in the previous centuries: "The European Village as Community: Origins and Functions," *Agricultural History*, XLV (1971), 157-78. For the context of urban social "seasons," see F. J. Fisher, "The Development of London as a Centre of Conspicuous Consumption in the Sixteenth and Seventeenth Centuries," *Transactions of the Royal Historical Society*, 4th series, 30 (1948), 37-50; E. A. Wrigley, "A Simple Model of London's Importance in Changing English Society and Economy 1650-1750," *Past & Present*, No. 37 (1967), 44-70; and David Maland, *Culture and Society in Seventeenth-Century France* (New York, 1970), esp. chapter 2.

starting in the early sixteenth century, they became involved in incessant turmoil, from food riots to rebellions. This is the unrest that Villari sees, perhaps rightly, as an indication of mounting social conflict and an endemic yearning for the restructuring of society. But the most spectacular and persistent expression of discontent was the outburst of witchcraft accusations. Many reasons have been advanced for these panics—the assault on magic by religious reformers, the disintegration of the close-knit face-to-face community, the intervention of central legal and political authorities, the intensification of social and economic conflicts at the local level—but they all come down to a recognition of the same set of circumstances: with familiar institutions and relationships disappearing, ordinary men and women lashed out against helpless neighbors whom they blamed for an unease they could not resolve. This period of recurrent disorder lasted, in its worst phase, for about a century, paralleling in the locality the tensions and unease that were apparent at all levels of society.[127]

Gradually, however, the forces of control were able to restore peace. In some areas the process was purely military. In Württemberg during the Thirty Years' War, for instance, the presence of troops helped dampen the ardor of witchcraft persecutions; fifty years later the *dragonnades* became the means of quelling peasant unruliness in France. Governments became more effective, too, in subduing the worst effects of economic disaster through food distribution and poor relief programs. Their intervention achieved its most remarkable success in the early eighteenth century, when a policy of isolation for the first time prevented the spread of plague from its port of entry into Europe, in this case Marseilles. Central administrations also perceived the social danger inherent in witchcraft panics, particularly when accusations escalated into the ranks of magistrates and public officials. Their efforts were thus increas-

127. Tilly, "Food Riot"; Thomas, *Magic;* Alan Macfarlane, *Witchcraft in Tudor and Stuart England: A Regional and Comparative Study* (New York, 1970); H. C. E. Midelfort, *Witch Hunting in Southwestern Germany, 1562-1684: The Social and Intellectual Foundations* (Stanford, 1972); and the literature surveyed in E. W. Monter, "The Historiography of European Witchcraft: Progress and Prospects," *Journal of Interdisciplinary History*, II (1972), 435-51.

ingly directed to restraining scapegoat fever rather than institution-alizing it through the legal system—a policy they had been inclined to follow earlier, when they were trying to bring all such local activity within uniform procedures. Both Reformation and Counter-Reformation ultimately had the same effect, narrowing the do-minion of magic and weaning parishioners away from a belief in supernatural powers outside the Church. Gradually, therefore, the witchcraft panics faded away; by the end of the seventeenth cen-tury, just as peasant revolts grew less frequent, so it became almost unheard of for a witch to be executed.[128]

The result (and to some extent the cause) was a renewal of calm in the countryside. Villagers were forced to adjust to new norms imposed from above, for a great seigneurial reaction—pursued by ever less accessible local lords—assured the restoration of a firm hierarchical order, possibly even more strictly formal than before. And the new aristocracies, particularly the recently risen bureau-crats, made sure that the mobility from which they had profited would cease to disturb their hard-won distinctiveness. Not surpris-ingly, there is the first indication in the late seventeenth century that upper class and bourgeois families were practicing birth con-trol on a broad scale—with the specific aim of defending their eco-nomic ascendancy. It is possible that families lower down on the social ladder were also occasionally limiting themselves, especially in times of hardship. If so, then they too were looking to the future and seeking to preserve their status, thus demonstrating yet again that changed conditions had been assimilated: that the ordinary people of the village were finally conforming to the transformations of daily life that had been thrust upon them during the previous two centuries.[129]

128. See the works cited in notes 126 and 127, above, and Robert Mandrou, *Magistrats et sorciers en France au XVIIe siècle* (Paris, 1968). On the 1720 plague, see Charles Carrière, M. Courdurié, and F. Rebuffat, *Marseille, ville morte: la peste de 1720* (Marseille, 1968). On poor relief, see Kamen, *Iron Century*, pp. 403-12, and the literature he cites on pp. 449-51.

129. In Blum's words, the increasingly poor peasants "adjusted to and ac-cepted the situation in which they found themselves" ("Village Com-munity," p. 515). See, too, G. Roupnel, *La Ville et la campagne au XVIIe siècle* (Paris, 1922) and Laszlo Revesz, *Der osteuropäische Bauer*

In the cities a process of adaptation was equally necessary. By 1700 there were once more, as there had not been since antiquity, urban concentrations whose populations approached and perhaps exceeded half a million. These areas were the supreme test of a government's ability to provide food for all its citizens, and there could be no doubt that the mechanisms that were developed proved equal to the task. Primitive systems of fresh water distribution were built; effective attention was given to fire-fighting and street lighting and cleaning; and the lines of supply to metropolises like London and Paris never broke down. Above all, by 1700 there could no longer be any question of cities acting independently of central regimes. The list of the seventeenth-century casualties in this struggle is long and distinguished: Barcelona, Bordeaux, Messina, Palermo, Naples, Amsterdam, the Hanseatic League, and Königsberg were merely the most famous of the victims. Yet the root of their subjugation was, paradoxically, the growing importance of economic activity, and hence of the need to give commerce a well-defined place in the development of the state. This process was much helped by the natural proclivity of merchants everywhere to look to their rulers for support and leadership—even where, as in Brandenburg-Prussia, they were hardly treated well in return. The consequent triumph of the mercantilist view, if not necessarily of mercantilist policies, signified the integration of cities into their countries to a degree that had been attained only exceptionally in previous centuries.[130] When at

---

(Bern, 1964). On birth control, see Louis Henry, *Anciennes Familles genevoises* (Paris, 1956); Louis Henry and Claude Lévy, "Ducs et pairs sous l'ancien régime: caractéristiques démographiques d'un caste," *Population*, XV (1960), 807-30; the articles in *La Prévention des naissances dans la famille* (Paris, 1960), esp. the one by Philippe Ariès on pp. 311-27; K. F. Helleiner, "New Light on the History of Urban Populations," *Journal of Economic History*, XVIII (1958), 56-61; and E. A. Wrigley, "Family Limitation in Pre-Industrial England," *Economic History Review*, 2nd series, XIX (1966), 82-109.

130. F. J. Fisher, "The Development of the London Food Market, 1540-1640," *Economic History Review*, V (1935), 46-64; Wrigley, "London's Importance"; J. W. Gough, *Sir Hugh Myddleton, Entrepreneur and Engineer* (Oxford, 1964), esp. chapters II-V on water distribution in London; and Ranum, *Paris*, esp. chapter 12: "The New Rome." Trevor-Roper, "General Crisis," p. 70, dates the subjugation of the

last, in the second half of the seventeenth century, wars came to be fought for economic advantage, the governmental-commercial alliance (the ancestor of the military-industrial complex) was not just sealed: it was cemented.

In the city as in the countryside, the chief fashioners and beneficiaries of the new co-operation were the highest levels of society, for this was a tranquillity established by the elite. Neither the small merchant nor the artisan, those rawest of recruits to the ranks of the literate, whose unrest had always been more radical and dangerous than the narrowly aimed rebellions of their country cousins, had any real say in the outcome. And once they had been abandoned by their superiors (as they were in all the revolts of the mid-century), none of these downtrodden groups could help but accede to the new status quo. After that, resignation and conformity came easily. Indeed, the enforced settlement that descended on the lower orders in their rural and urban localities was the exact counterpart to the stabilization that at this very time was appearing in the more visible arenas of political relations and elite religious beliefs.

The next great period of advance, both economically and demographically, was to come in the mid-eighteenth century, and it is natural to speculate on the links that might be drawn between the situation that has been described here and that next leap forward, which was to render pallid even the achievements of the sixteenth century. One hypothesis that seems plausible, though it is entirely

---

cities before the sixteenth century. Yet the Hanseatic League was not dissolved until the seventeenth century, and most of the cities mentioned here had to be besieged or sternly intimidated by their monarchs and princes after 1640. It might be noted that the great exception that proved the rule, Geneva, remained independent because its hinterland was not the surrounding countryside but international Calvinism. The hypothesis posited below, in the last two paragraphs of this section, about the linkage between a calming down and the resumed growth of the eighteenth century, owes much to conversations I have had with E. A. Wrigley—from whose comments I have profited throughout this section. I might add that one other major source of calm and resumed growth, the gradual disappearance of plague and subsistence crises, seems to have been the accelerator, rather than the originator, of this renewal, for it did not become noticeable until the second quarter of the eighteenth century.

tentative and will require much research to evaluate, is that the very calming down paved the way for the later expansions—the renewed security was the pre-condition for the resumption of rapid economic and demographic advance. In a time of stability a revived feeling of confidence could grow, for while those staid mollifiers, Fleury and Walpole, ruled the major powers of Europe, allowing an aura of solidity and familiarity to return to the Continent, the forces could gather strength that were to precipitate the all-encompassing revolutions of the late eighteenth century. Every age of course contains the seeds of its heir, but in this case the succession may have taken a peculiar form: the coming-to-terms with the upheavals that had been launched around 1500 may have inspired the very assurance out of which a new round of startling growth and innovation could emerge.

The sequence in economics and population trends thus lends a different context to the changes in politics, religion, and thought than that which Hobsbawm proposed. It is less of a causative agent (though it has some of that character), and more a general accelerator or reflector of events in other spheres of life. The whirlwind advances of the sixteenth century were certainly potent sources of the prevailing unease, as was the deceleration that followed. And the end of the boom, by closing one safety valve, may well have hastened the political explosions of the mid-seventeenth century. Thereafter, however, it was the revival of governmental authority that relieved or repressed social tensions, and at least indirectly paved the way for further economic and demographic growth, rather than the other way around. Nothing essential in Europe's commerce or industry had changed (capitalism had made no striking gains at the expense of feudalism), but much of the generalized uncertainty and anxiety had dissipated as the peoples of the Continent came to accept the new structures—economic, governmental, geographic, and social—that dominated their lives. In the village, just as at Court, some measure of relaxation, of acquiescence, was once again possible.

X

RESOLUTION IN AESTHETICS

As this analysis began with high culture, with the reactions and expressions of the most literate and sensitive members of society, so must it end there. To the extent that this is an essay about perception, in which the discussion of mounting uncertainties, then strivings, then resolutions, centers on changing *attitudes*, sometimes even unsupported by changing realities, it is essential that the final and most decisive stage, the sense of settlement, be clearly visible in the contrasts between early and late seventeenth-century culture.

And here the picture is, indeed, unmistakable. For the titanic struggles of the generations from Shakespeare to Milton gave way almost suddenly to genteelness and calm. The confidence that the Baroque exuded but never quite captured was replaced by the much more convincing assurance of the last decades of the century, when artists felt less driven to trumpet their powers, when they ceased protesting too much. The tempestuous grandeur of literature, painting, and sculpture had been an attempt to belie the words of doubt and uncertainty that lay beneath. Now room-sized canvases and heroic poetry became decreasingly necessary as the impulse to overwhelm doubt dwindled away. It was as if the soaring problems of human existence, whose treatment had required such dramatic flair and epic scale, no longer excited the imagination. Searching, emotional questions were simply losing their appeal as Europe began to calm down: resolution had been reached, and hence "crisis" was past.

In the fields of poetry and drama the divide is relatively sharp, as the helter-skelter plots of a Shakespeare or a Lope de Vega, roaming all over the kaleidoscopes of human existence, give way to a more formal aesthetic. That the dominant genre of late seventeenth- and eighteenth-century playwriting in England should have been

Restoration Comedy surely establishes the point beyond doubt. Moreover, this reorientation was confirmed by the requirements laid down by Boileau, whose *Art poétique* was the chief guide to literary taste in the last years of the century; the most important virtue of poetry, in his view, was its craftsmanship, not its appeal to the emotions. And the results speak for themselves: between the massive stateliness of Milton and the deft charm of Dryden lies a world of difference. Nor was the change lost on the poets themselves. They considered it impossible to follow Milton's footsteps, not only because of his stature, but because the enterprise he had been engaged in seemed to have lost its urgency. "The force of nature could no farther go," wrote Dryden,[131] and Marvell summed up the prevailing sentiment in the year of Milton's death:

> Pardon me, Mighty Poet, nor despise
> My causeless, yet not impious surmise.
> But I am now convinced, and none will dare
> Within thy labors to pretend a share.
> Thou hast not missed one thought that could be fit,
> And all that was improper dost omit:
> So that no room is here for writers left,
> But to detect their ignorance or theft.[132]

Perhaps not until Blake did English verse recapture Milton's soaring passion.

In Spain this intensity made its last appearance in the drama of Calderón; in Germany in the generation of Opitz, Gryphius, and Gerhardt. And in France, the new cynosure of Europe, the imposition of stable forms was the central theme of the history of taste. Appropriately, it was Racine, the exemplar of the triumph of formality, who crystallized the progression that had taken place when he delivered the obituary eulogy of Corneille to the Académie Française:

> You know in what a condition the stage was when he began to write. . . . All the rules of art, and even those of decency and decorum, broken everywhere. . . . Corneille, after having for

131. *Lines on Milton*, line 5.
132. *On Mr. Milton's Paradise Lost*, lines 23-30.

some time sought the right path and struggled against the bad taste of his day, inspired by extraordinary genius and helped by the study of the ancients, at last brought reason upon the stage.[133]

This remarkable aesthetic credo, with its emphasis on decorum and its indifference to Corneille's own attachment to "bad taste" when his masterpiece, *Le Cid*, brought down on him the wrath of the Académie, traces exactly the transformation that had taken place in the commitments of the creative artist.

Now it is true that the formalization of drama prevented neither Corneille nor Racine from plumbing the depths of human emotion. In this respect the chasm between Racine and his contemporaries across the Channel, Farquhar and Vanbrugh, could not have been wider. But this contrast should not lead us to assume that nothing had really changed. There was, first, the underlying common interest of both sets of playwrights in manners, an inclination they shared with such earlier contemporaries as Molière and the authors of masques. For all of Phèdre's blazing torment, she retained an unwavering attachment to the norms of conduct:

> Mad that I am, where do my senses lead me?
> What do I say? Where do I let my soul
> and my desires stray? I've lost my mind!

she exclaimed as she awakened to the full implications of her own desires. And when she banished Hyppolite

> . . . then I breathed at last. When he was gone my days ran smoothly once again.[134]

The concern for behavior, for the rules and conventions of conduct, was as overriding in the late seventeenth century as it had

133. Jean Racine, "Discours prononcé à l'Académie Française à la réception de M. de Corneille (1685)," *Oeuvres de J. Racine,* ed. Paul Mesnard, IV (Paris, 1886), p. 366. My translation. This assessment delicately echoes that of Giorgio Vasari on Giotto: "Giotto alone, in a rude and inept age, when all good methods of art had long been lost, dead and buried in the ruins of war, set out upon the path that may be called the true one." *Lives of the Painters* (New York, 1946), p. 16.
134. *Racine, Phaedra: A Translation,* trans. B. D. N. Grebanier (Great Neck, 1958), pp. 13 and 20.

been subordinate in the age of Shakespeare. Even Molière, the master observer of manners, encountered disapproval when he made the mistake of having his actors speak the lines of Corneille's *Nicomède* like ordinary people, not aristocrats.

With that said, one must still admit that the differences between *Phèdre* and *The Recruiting Officer* far outweigh their similarities. Obeisance to manners cannot, on its own, determine their equivalence. Yet it is also clear—and this is the main reason to believe a change had taken place—that the future lay with Restoration Comedy and its ilk, not with the ascetic purity of Racine. As in politics, the cut-off points are never absolute, and there are after-tremors to disturb the general subsidence. But one cannot dismiss the coincidence that the last of the titans, Milton, Corneille, and Racine, all finished producing their epic verses during the 1670's, in fact within a five-year period (though Racine, having turned, like Calderón, to religion, did write two last plays, in 1689 and 1691). After 1677, the date of *Phèdre*, outbursts of passionate feeling became ever more exceptional. Bunyan and Swift were final echoes, lost amidst a welter of delicacy and frivolity: the ethic of "sensibility and fine feeling" that Laurence Sterne surveyed so accurately in *A Sentimental Journey* nearly a hundred years later.

The arbiters of taste were encouraging this relaxation in a number of ways. Most important was the rise of salons and academies. By its very nature, the salon put a premium on surface qualities: quickness, wit, charm, and a slightly cynical attitude toward the world. That the great catch of a Parisian salon should have been the deservedly forgotten poet Voiture, and not Corneille, speaks volumes about the character of the intellectual exchange that the institution promoted.[135] And the obsession with forms and rules that animated the great academies, notably the Académie Française, had similar consequences. They became engrossed in questions of style, rather than content; their very aim was to prevent or to moderate relapses into vulgar excess. In this respect, the rise of classicism, however much it may have inspired the work of Milton, Corneille, and Racine, was in the long run a means of formalizing expression and reducing literature's capacity for fervor.

135. Maland, *Culture and Society*, pp. 47 and 53-54.

Exactly the same succession emerges from painting, where the profundity and strenuous aspirations of Baroque gave way to the elegance and grace of Rococo. Between the power and exuberance of Rubens, Hals, or Bernini, and the wistfulness of Watteau, there is another of these momentous shifts in feeling and taste. The writing was on the wall when Bernini came to Paris in the 1660's to design a new wing for the Louvre, only to find that he had to tone down and simplify his designs, ostensibly to save money but also to meet different standards of taste. When, in the end, Perrault undertook the commission, the result was, in the words of a recent student of the affair, "a dramatic repudiation of the baroque."[136] And this incident was symptomatic of a much larger change. The great themes, the swirling drama, that energized the works of Rubens and his contemporaries, had metamorphosed by the end of the century into the sweet, genteel, and ornate world of aristocratic Courts; bright colors had given way to pastels.

The boundaries are even less crisp in painting than they are in literature, because the first indications of the changed aesthetic are in the canvases Claude Lorrain produced before mid-century, yet the quintessential Baroque master, Bernini, survived almost to his eighty-second birthday in 1680. It is noteworthy, too, that Le Brun was still at work in the 1690's, a few years before Watteau emerged as the leading figure at Versailles. But these overlaps do not hide the essential lessening of tension that took place. Although there is a splendid dignity in Le Brun's creations, such as his *Chancellor Séguier* (fig. 8), as there is in much of the portraiture of this last third of the seventeenth century, it is evident that the pictures by his contemporaries, certainly those by Claude, and by successors like Watteau, were gradually being scaled down to the size of a salon; their canvases, increasingly smaller than the ambitious paintings the Baroque produced, would have looked absurd on immense

136. *Ibid.*, p. 250. The Bernini design is reproduced in Plate 24, opposite p. 145. See, too, V.-L. Tapié, *Baroque et classicisme* (Paris, 1957). The fullest elaboration of the change in style that occurred around 1650, in this case in Italian painting, is Nikolaus Pevsner, *Barockmalerei in den romanischer Ländern,* Part 1 of *Die italienische Malerei vom Ende der Renaissance bis zum ausgehenden Rokoko* (Potsdam, 1928), pp. 193 ff.

(photo: Service de Documentation Photographique de la Réunion des Musées Nationaux)

8. Le Brun *Chancellor Séguier* Louvre Museum, Paris

walls. Their atmosphere, too, was appropriate for the salon: idyllic and relaxed scenes, occasionally melancholic but never agitated. An era more committed to weighty content would have found it incredible that Claude could depict the scene of the angel appearing to Hagar when she was dying of thirst as taking place in a landscape dominated by a lake (fig. 9). In Claude's *Sermon on the Mount* (fig. 10), Christ is almost invisible, while the tense scene of *Moses before the Burning Bush* vanishes into an indistinct corner of a distant landscape.

Earlier painters, most notably Rembrandt, had certainly been capable of portraying peaceful, tender subjects, but at the same time they had not been able to resist undertaking the most stirring themes. Significantly, though, the latter gradually receded in the oeuvre of the great Dutchman. As H. W. Janson has described it, Rembrandt's "work from the mid-1620's to the early 1640's, with its emphasis on dramatic display, differs markedly from that of the 1650's and 1660's, which is gently lyrical and introspective."[137] And the withdrawal from the grandiose suffuses the paintings of those other mid-century masters, Claude and Vermeer. That such a preference should have appeared now, after over 120 years of Mannerism and Baroque when one can search for it in vain, and that it should have grown pre-eminent within another generation, is striking testimony to the transformation wrought in the mid-seventeenth century. The goals were so much more limited that one is tempted to speak of the departure of the giants. Even the revival of classicism had produced a genius of awesome power, Poussin, before the mode had become ritualized, as in literature, and an encouragement to formality and restraint. The deaths of Rubens, Van Dyck, Velázquez, Poussin, Hals, and Rembrandt, all within less than thirty years between the 1640's and 1660's, mark the passing, not merely of a style, but of an attitude toward the very purposes of

137. H. W. Janson, "The Image of Man in 17th and 18th Century Art," in Mortimer Chambers et al., *The Western Experience* (New York, 1974), adjoining plate 40. For a specific discussion of the "triumph of reason at the expense of emotion" in Dutch art in this period, see J. G. Van Gelder, "Two Aspects of the Dutch Baroque. Reason and Emotion," *De Artibus Opuscula. XL: Essays in Honor of Erwin Panofsky*, ed. Millard Meiss, Vol. I (New York, 1961), pp. 445-53.

art. Henceforth painting was to be pleasing rather than exciting, decorative rather than powerful.

What is obvious from the foregoing is that the elite and its most creative minds were placing different demands on literary and artistic expression. No longer torn by doubts and huge aspirations, they felt that the distressing problems of the previous century and a half had been resolved, that the disruptive forces launched around 1500 had at last been assimilated, and that now they could relax. The sense of settlement induced a preference for calm enjoyment and sunny pleasures that writers and painters satisfied with aplomb. Light humor and elaborate decoration suited the new mood perfectly, and it was appropriate that clothing, too, became more ornate after the 1650's. Yet still the question arises, as it has in earlier sections of this essay: had Europe's situation changed in any definable way, or did some people just *think* it had changed? Was there tangible justification for the renewal of confidence, and hence for the altered canons of taste? In intellectual life there would seem to have been an authentic breakthrough of this kind, the triumph of science, which did produce genuine solutions for major problems. But a more detailed examination reveals that the connection is not quite so simple.

*   *   *

If any activity of the sixteenth and seventeenth centuries represented a quest for authority and certainty, it was science. From the first overturnings of traditional systems, whether the physics of Aristotle, the astronomy of Ptolemy, or the anatomy of Galen, until the final recognition in those same fields of the validity of the theories of Bacon, Kepler, Galileo, Descartes, Harvey, and Newton, the perennial search was for solid truths that would be acceptable to all. And it was apparent that, by their efforts, the scientists were contributing both to the confusion that was so noticeable in the late sixteenth and the early seventeenth century, and to the great strivings that constituted the response to the resultant malaise. Yet in the end their solutions to their epistemological doubts paved the way for the creation of a new epistemology in the late seventeenth century. One can recognize, therefore, that the parallels with developments in other areas were close, and that during the first stage of competing theories the scientists were a major source of the contra-

9. Claude *The Angel Appearing to Hagar* National Gallery, London

o. Claude *The Sermon on the Mount* The Frick Collection, New York

dictions that caused so much perplexity in the generations of Montaigne, Donne, and Descartes. But it is not equally clear that their subsequent consensus was the origin of Europe's renewed assurance. To substantiate that view, I must present the case in some detail. And for the initial ambiguous assault on the ancients I can do no better than to quote the recent overview by Theodore Brown, an historian of science:

> Copernicus criticized Ptolemaic cosmology, only to follow Ptolemy in the intricate details of planetary theory. Vesalius condemned Galen for resorting to simian instead of human dissection, and then demonstrated at every turn, usually without saying so, just how his own physiology remained Galenic. Cesalpino, a medical writer midway between Vesalius and William Harvey, asserted the great philosophical superiority of Aristotle to Galen, and then discovered that as one consequence of doing so he left no important function to the multitude of veins in the human body; he thus seemed to point to a new theory of blood flow that was consistent with neither ancient system of physiology. Harvey advanced circulation as the theory which accounted for Cesalpino's and other anomalous discoveries of the sixteenth century, boldly "cast his die" with theoretical innovation, but then sharply turned back to Aristotle, and perhaps the Hermetics, for an explanation of why and how blood circulation worked as it did. Kepler investigated mathematical formulas and geometrical curves to put into order the data of post-Copernican astronomy, but he pursued his investigations from within a Neoplatonic and animistic framework. Young Galileo explored the perplexing problems of motion, and though he recognized that Aristotle was wrong at almost every turn, he could only think to resort to the "divine Archimedes" for guidance to alternate formulations of kinematics.[138]

The result, of course, was to add fuel to the belief that certainty could never be restored.

Gradually, these conflicts began to crystallize into a struggle between the proponents of vast systems—an "energetic, angry, confusing" clash between ancients and moderns, between corpuscularists and Hermeticists, between Copernicans and Ptolemaics and

138. "Comment": paper delivered to the American Historical Association convention in New Orleans, December 28, 1972, pp. 2-3.

Braheians, between Cartesians and Baconians, all in the name of "right method." This effusion of "competing methodological and metaphysical formulations . . . in plethora"[139] was the equivalent of the grandiose ambitions we have seen to be characteristic of so much of the first half of the seventeenth century. Their very diversity only worsened the malaise, but that deterioration proved to be —here as elsewhere—the storm before the calm.

For almost as suddenly as it had started the turmoil began to die away. Even before Newton put the capstone on the revolution, and even before the resolution of the final conflict between Newtonianism and Cartesianism, scientists had coalesced around a new and firm approach to knowledge: "Robert Hooke in England, Christian Huygens in France, Jan Swammerdam in Holland, and Marcello Malpighi in Italy all learned how to combine 'Baconian' experimental methods with the corpuscular view of mechanical macrocosm and microcosm. Hermetic and Mosaical alternatives were condemned as atavistic unorthodoxies and excluded from the new, settled consensus of orthodox mechanical/experimental science."[140] With reviving confidence, scientists organized their efforts through learned societies and journals, and presented to the world around them the very model of epistemological assurance.

The response of elite culture at large was direct and almost immediate. For here was the principle of radical doubt being put to marvelous advantage, transformed from a curse into a blessing. The old, shaky reliance on tradition as the root of knowledge had been replaced with an emphasis on abstract reasoning and sense experience. That scientists did not, in fact, follow the neat progression of observation-generalization-test which Locke later described as

139. *Ibid.*, p. 3. For the most notorious of these conflicts, involving Galileo and the Inquisition, see the works by Santillana and Cochrane cited in notes 67 and 117, above. Cochrane's is one of the very few studies that connect scientific thought with the larger social and economic background. For other examples, see Charles Webster, ed., *The Intellectual Revolution of the Seventeenth Century* (London, 1974), P. M. Rattansi, "The Helmontian-Galenist Controversy in Restoration England," *Ambix*, XII (1964), 1-23, and Theodore M. Brown, "The College of Physicians and the Acceptance of Iatromechanism in England, 1665-1695," *Bulletin of the History of Medicine*, XLIV (1970), 12-30.

140. "Comment," p. 4.

proper scientific procedure was less important than the belief that they *did* behave in this fashion. For many who could not really understand what Galileo had been talking about in *The Two New Sciences,* or the full implications of Descartes's work, science nonetheless seemed to offer—because of its own assurance, if for no other reason—the answer to baffling problems of epistemology and authority. It no longer mattered that earlier truths were under fire; now there was something better to put in their stead, at least in studies of nature. And if this was possible in one field, why not in all fields?

The quick and decisive triumph of this handful of scientists is one of the most amazing episodes in European history. By the middle of the seventeenth century, aristocrats and virtuosi were lionizing them and trying uncomprehendingly to imitate them, setting up little observatories and herbariums in their gardens, installing talking statues in their living rooms, or describing sand dunes in the hope that this could add to the sum of scientific knowledge. Less than thirty years after Galileo's condemnation the two most powerful kings in Europe blessed scientific institutions with royal charters, and soon an academy became an essential ornament for a self-respecting Court. The office and the knighthood bestowed on Newton, and the statues raised in his honor, may have merely fulfilled the recommendations Bacon had made a century earlier, but in fact such rewards would have seemed virtually inconceivable just a few decades before they were granted.[141]

Moreover, the attempts to appropriate the new discoveries domi-

---

141. Walter E. Houghton, Jr., "The English Virtuoso in the Seventeenth Century," *Journal of the History of Ideas,* III (1942), 51-73 and 190-219; A. R. Hall and M. B. Hall, eds., *The Correspondence of Henry Oldenburg,* IV: *1667-1668* (Madison, 1967), pp. 513-16; Bacon, *New Organon,* p. 117. A significant testimony to the new stature of science came at the end of the century from Geneva, whose Academy was slowly adapting to Cartesianism. Faced by a major crisis in the 1690's because of a drop in enrollments following the Revocation of the Edict of Nantes, one reformer suggested as a remedy that the Academy establish a Chair of Mathematics, because students now expected an education in such matters. See Michael Heyd, *Cartesianism, Secularization, and Academic Reform: Jean Robert Chouet and the Academy of Geneva, 1669-1704* (unpub. Ph.D. diss., Princeton, 1974), chapter VII.

nated most areas of intellectual life. Metaphysical inquiry, whose most prominent figures were Descartes, Spinoza, Leibniz, and Locke, revolved around the most appropriate applications of scientific principles to cosmology and epistemology. Political theory went through similar explorations, particularly in the work of Hobbes, whose mathematical and mechanistic reasoning derived directly from his acquaintance with scientific literature. The cult of reason; the assertions of order in the universe; the vanquishing of the "ancients" in the Battle of the Books; the new theories that reigned in subjects as far apart as the building of fortifications, the planning of gardens, and the study of populations; all took their justification from the successes of science. Pascal was the last major figure to warn against this idolization; significantly, his reservations remained unfashionable for over a century.[142]

There has been considerable interest in the question of why this sweeping turnaround happened. And at first sight it seems that the comfortable Whiggish hypothesis of the scientists triumphing because they were right could give us the key to an understanding of the general settlement of the late seventeenth century. The truth will out, according to this view, and all will be well. But the interpretation flounders in face of the continuing tension within science between two somewhat antithetical schools, the Newtonian/Baconian and the Cartesian, and in face of the very different understanding of scientific advance that we owe to Thomas Kuhn.[143] It is clear that the scientists themselves had been driven by the need to find convincing answers after becoming dissatisfied with old ones; that their acceptance of specific models was often irrational; and that in any case laymen who admired them rarely knew exactly what had been demonstrated. Solutions did not emerge overnight, with everybody suddenly agreeing that one theory was right. Quite the contrary: the victory of a single, accepted orthodoxy (in this case Newtonianism) was a slow and painful process, lasting far into the eighteenth century.

142. In Hazard's words, "Pascal . . . had no disciples" (*European Mind*, p. 144). The famous attack by Voltaire epitomized the eighteenth century's dismissal of Pascal's concerns.
143. Thomas S. Kuhn, *The Structure of Scientific Revolutions* (Chicago, 1962).

Equally problematical for the Whiggish hypothesis is the incipient decline of scientific work in the generation of its greatest achievements. To quote Brown again:

> In Italy the Accademia del Cimento disbanded in 1667 after but ten years' existence; in England at about the same time the Royal Society experienced a drastic decline in membership and an attendant disaster in its finances; and across Europe generally physicians, who for a decade or two had been among the most eager recruits to scientific activities, began heading back, usually at a rapid pace, to the greater certainty and security of medical practice. By the 1670's Thomas Shadwell could write *The Virtuoso* as a satire on the gentleman amateur of science, and this play is but one among many contemporary expressions of bemused detachment about that new thing called science. And need one even add mention of Seth Ward, John Wilkins and others who had earlier been pioneers and advocates of the new science but who now turned to comfortable careers as well-placed Churchmen?[144]

One can add to this catalogue the drift of Royal Societies toward a role as havens for the socially ambitious rather than as centers of serious research, and the striking slackening of scientific progress during the first half of the eighteenth century.[145]

One is thus driven to the conclusion that the triumph of science was as much a symptom as a cause of the wave of settlement of the late seventeenth century. Society took Newton and Locke to its heart primarily because they offered a far less troubling and difficult message than did Descartes or Pascal or Hobbes—none of whom, after all, had been inherently less impressive or "scientific" in their arguments. What the age wanted to hear was that the world was harmonious and sensible; that human beings were marvelously capable, endowed with an orderly Reason that could solve all problems. Believing that their problems had indeed *been* solved, contem-

---

144. "Comment," pp. 7-8. See, too, my "Puritanism and the Rise of Experimental Science in England," *Journal of World History*, VII (1962), 46-67.

145. M. 'Espinasse, "The Decline and Fall of Restoration Science," *Past & Present*, No. 14 (1958), 71-89; Eric Ashby, *Technology and the Academics* (London, 1958), pp. 1-66; and my "Puritanism," which also documents the statements about Bacon in the last paragraph of this section.

poraries demanded an epistemology that would allow them to relax and enjoy life, and this was exactly the soothing reassurance Locke provided. The profound doubts and questionings evaporated, to be replaced by a smug confidence that took even such disasters as the famines and devastations of 1709 in its stride, and comfortably ignored such awkward prickers of conscience as Bunyan, Vauban, or Swift. Their literature and art revealed that people wanted to be pleased and entertained, not stirred; their heroes, therefore, had to confirm their newly found pride and contentment over man's capacity for solving fractious problems. Newton met these requirements so admirably that soon Alexander Pope could feel justified in comparing his achievements to those of God on the first day of creation. Without detracting from the brilliance of Sir Isaac's accomplishments, one can still admit that his genius was not unmatched in all history; yet the reaction to his writings *was* unique. One must conclude, therefore, that it was the need he and his colleagues filled, rather than the compelling force of their insights, that prompted such serene and total adoration.

Lest it be thought that such an interpretation of intellectual change is implausible precisely because it seems to have no parallel, I might cite the very similar mechanism that worked in favor of another Englishman a few decades earlier. I am referring, of course, to the triumph of Francis Bacon in the 1640's, twenty years after he had been reviled and disgraced by some of the very men who now adopted his philosophy—for the simple reason that his ideas, long in limbo, accorded with their new program as leaders of a revolution. The circumstances, not the ideas themselves, were decisive. And once the hero was found, the questions that hovered about him—in Bacon's case his political career, in Newton's case such scientific problems as the ether and the cause of gravity—were safely ignored amid the torrent of adulation.

XI

POSSIBLE EXPLANATIONS:
THE EFFECTS OF WAR

Where, at the end of this whirlwind tour of two hundred years of European history, can we find the explanation for the discontinuity that has been our central concern? The presence of the discontinuity can surely not be denied. The transition from the age of Reformation to the age of Enlightenment should no longer be mysterious, and the distinctiveness and homogeneity of the period from the death of Calvin to the birth of Voltaire should be apparent. To return to the contrasts posed as the beginning of this essay, we can appreciate that, on one side of the divide, Rubens, Milton, Charles I, Condé in the 1640's, Wallenstein, Galileo, Descartes, Hobbes, Gustavus Adolphus, Paul V, and a witch-ridden society were all engaged, in a setting where all standards and institutions were open to question and total overhaul, in correspondingly vast ambitions—to overwhelm the senses, to change the forms of politics, to find a new order, and to control or evade unresolvable doubts. On the other side of the divide stand those who either established, or worked within, a structure that was no longer bitterly disputed—for whom the uncertainties had essentially been settled, possibilities had been limited, and relaxation had become more attainable: Claude, Dryden, Charles II, Condé in the 1680's, Eugène, Newton, Locke, Charles XII, Innocent XI, and a witch-free (or at least relatively impervious) society. The major division that occurred approximately in the third quarter of the seventeenth century between disequilibrium and equilibrium may have been the result of massive delusion, but it was real nevertheless. And it is from the phenomenon of resolution that we can deduce Europe's passage through a "crisis": a "crisis" so general that it affected all forms of human activity, from diplomacy to drama, and every country, from Russia to Portugal; a "crisis" primarily in perception, although it had its material components; and a "crisis" of authority, if a single label seems appropriate to such disparate manifestations.

Still, however, we are left with the reason behind it all. Why people should have been so disturbed, so anxious to find new assurance, is fairly evident in the wake of the events around 1500. But there is no obvious answer to the riddle of why they stopped struggling with these difficulties, why they should have determined to put an end to the challenges, the dissensions, the fears. A number of real decisions were reached, it is true: Westphalia, the collapse of the Cromwellian revolution and the Fronde, the law of universal gravitation. But the fundamental question is why they seemed so decisive; and why, when many areas, such as aesthetics, experienced no such moments of truth, the transformation, the willingness to mute the striving, was nevertheless so universal and so easily absorbed. Is there anything in the immediately preceding period that suggests why the resolution came, and why at this particular time?

The simplest answer would be sheer exhaustion. And there is an element of plain weariness in the acceptance of new frameworks in the late seventeenth century: the grand gesture could be sustained only so long. Similarly, one could argue that the decisive shift, which made all the other stabilizations possible, was the decline of religious fervor as an influence on public affairs. But these hypotheses hardly solve our difficulty, for we still have to ask "why now?" Why did it happen in the middle of the seventeenth century and not fifty years earlier or later? Why did the response to religious extremism not change in the 1590's rather than the 1650's? No explanation will be effective unless it can reveal some crucial influence, or set of influences, that belongs to roughly the second quarter of the seventeenth century.

A number of possibilities present themselves. One is the likelihood that, upon reaching a sufficient degree of ubiquity and control, bureaucracies became an irresistible instrument of restraint. The advantage of such a "critical mass" theory would be its comprehensiveness, for it would relate equally to both sides of the divide between absolutism and constitutionalism. But its relevance to intellectual change seems tenuous, and there is the additional difficulty that bureaucratization advanced unevenly in Europe's countries during the seventeenth century, suffusing some far more than others.

A second, and more widely applicable possibility is suggested by the aristocracy's almost universal domination of politics, society, and culture in the late seventeenth century, a continent-wide ascent symbolized by the career of Eugène. Whether aristocrats were brought to a newly powerful position in central governments and social institutions by the imperious behest of a monarch (as in Peter's Russia), or by a mutually beneficial alliance with a king (as in Louis XIV's France and Leopold I's Austria), or by their own exertions (as in Sweden and England), the results were essentially the same. Badly frightened by the dangerously subversive implications (and occasional accomplishments) of the turmoil that shook Europe at mid-century, the traditional nobility closed ranks, rejected its former disruptive ambitions, and determinedly reimposed the order it had helped undermine. To the extent that the period from about 1660 to 1789 was the age of the aristocracy *par excellence*—a time when the great landowners and courtiers, secure, confident, and relaxed in their supremacy, could enjoy untroubled the victory of deference and the status quo—the fundamental shift from turbulence to calm was primarily their work. They were the ones who benefited most from the new situation, gaining privilege, office, status, and wealth without the usual concomitants of aggressive, suspicious, and destructive confrontations. Consequently, since they had achieved their ends peacefully in the aftermath of unrest, it was overwhelmingly in their interest (and in their power) to defuse whatever tensions remained.

Another book would be necessary to work out the mechanism whereby this process unfolded: to trace the changing roles and attitudes of Europe's aristocracies, to follow the redirection of their political and cultural influence as they "captured" centralized governments, and to explain why the changes occurred. In the remainder of this essay I can but outline one of the developments that contributed decisively to the transformation—namely, the revulsion against the brutal excesses of the Thirty Years' War. One cannot attribute the more acquiescent and settled atmosphere of the subsequent period to this single reaction alone, and indeed I have just suggested other possible causes; but from this perspective the major turning-point is unmistakable, and moreover it can be documented with graphic and dramatic evidence. By exploring its features even briefly, therefore, we can obtain some insight into the reasons for the vast reorientation that ensued.

*   *   *

There is no doubt that, to concerned observers, the disintegrations of the Thirty Years' War, the frightful specter of total anarchy raised by the new military tactics, the unprecedented slaughter, and the lawlessnes of international relations, seemed to have brought Europe to the edge of the abyss. The shock of the unbridled chaos, of a myriad of competing claims battling each other to extinction, made thoughtful men realize that these reckless assertions of private will were the surest route to disaster. Pascal's brief dialogue summed up the dreadful consequences of totally relative thinking:

"Why are you killing me for your own benefit? I am unarmed."

"Why, do you not live on the other side of the water? My friend, if you lived on this side, I should be a murderer, but since you live on the other side, I am a brave man and it is right."[146]

And Locke, whose childhood was spent under the shadow of the Continental war, even though he lived beyond its reach in England, drew on his vivid memory of it as the original impulse for his advocacy of religious toleration. He remembered, he wrote, the "perpetual foundation of war and contention, all those flames that have made such havoc and desolation in Europe, and have not been quenched but with the blood of so many millions."[147]

146. *Pensées*, trans. Krailsheimer, p. 44. In the midst of his brief but brilliant description of the great transformation that marked the seventeenth century, a description that epitomizes part of the argument of this essay, Trevor-Roper dismisses the impact of war as the prime explanation for the "crisis" ("General Crisis," pp. 61-63). He suggests that the wars of 1618-59 did not differ from their predecessors and hence were no more influential. I trust that the pages that follow will substantiate both their distinctiveness and their decisiveness—not in stimulating a "crisis" but in precipitating a resolution.

147. Locke, *Two Tracts*, ed. Abrams, p. 160. For similar sentiments, expressed in the same period, see the sermons by William [?Gilbert]

Hobbes' state of nature drew inspiration from the same source, as did Locke's. But it was the Germans themselves who expressed the horror most plaintively. The familiar figure of the Beast of War, devouring all in his path, dominated the broadsides; and the prophecies of doom emanated from Gerhardt's pen:

> We are brutally beaten by a rod strong and hard,
> And yet we must ask "who has given us this reward?"
>   . . .
> Oh, come on! Wake up, wake up, you hard world, open your eyes,
> Before terror comes upon you in swift, sudden surprise.[148]

Most shattering of all was Grimmelshausen, whose descriptions of the war only confirmed what many knew. The following was one incident among dozens:

> [The soldiers] stretched the hired man out flat on the ground, stuck a wooden wedge in his mouth to keep it open, and emptied a milk bucket full of stinking manure drippings down his throat; they called it a Swedish cocktail. . . . Then they used thumb-screws, which they cleverly made out of their pistols, to torture the peasants. . . . They put one of the captured hayseeds in the bake-oven and lighted a fire in it. They put a rope around someone else's head and tightened it like a tourniquet until blood came out of his mouth, nose, and ears. In short, every soldier had his favorite method of making life miserable for peasants, and every peasant had his own misery. . . . I can't say much about the captured wives, hired girls, and daughters because the soldiers didn't let me watch their doings. But I do remember hearing pitiful screams from various dark corners.[149]

Sheldon, John Bramhall, and Richard Baxter in *In God's Name: Examples of Preaching in England from the Act of Supremacy to the Act of Uniformity, 1534-1662*, ed. John Chandos (Indianapolis, 1971), pp. 544 and 550-54. I owe this reference to Alan Kors. Milton's "all this waste of wealth, and loss of blood" is in the same tradition.

148. Quoted in Gebhardt, ed., *Handbuch der deutschen Geschichte*, II, p. 197. My translation.

149. J. J. C. von Grimmelshausen, *Simplicius Simplicissimus*, trans. George Schulz-Behrend (Indianapolis, 1965), p. 10.

Every war produces such excesses, of course. The longing for peace in France in the 1590's was no less than the yearnings of the Germans in the 1630's and 1640's. But none of the wars of the previous centuries had been so persistent and so totally destructive of human life for so long a period and over so wide an area. We have already quoted Michael Roberts' description of the new intensity and scale of war; the following is his comment on the reaction to the Thirty Years' War that took hold in military circles: "an age of reason and mathematical logic would try to bring war itself within the scope of its calculations, to the detriment of that offensive spirit without which wars cannot be won."[150] Although armies continued to grow, their viciousness and spoliation declined—a unique reversal that signifies how deeply the European conscience had been seared by the events of the 1620's to 1640's. The momentum that the violence built up had been so powerful that it took two years after the signing of the peace to bring the serious skirmishing to an end, and another four years to persuade soldiers to return home from their garrisons and to end their state of readiness.[151] No wonder it seemed that the avalanche of combat might shatter European society beyond recall, or that the relief at its end should have been immense enough to change the nature of warfare: to end, for a while, the "swath of destruction" policy enunciated by Gustavus.

The changes that followed have been seen as a "restriction of violence" that helped form modern industrial society.[152] For there is general scholarly agreement that war became "milder" and "more civilized" in the late seventeenth century, and that particular credit must go to the improvement of discipline, military academies, and the creation of standing armies. According to Louis André, the army fashioned by Le Tellier and Louvois could not have been more different, in its acquiescence to regulation, from the "dis-

---

150. "The Military Revolution," p. 203.
151. Wedgwood, *Thirty Years War*, pp. 485-90.
152. John U. Nef, *Cultural Foundations of Industrial Civilization* (New York, 1960), esp. chapters III and V. This book stresses the disenchantment with violence, which Nef sees as a basic theme of the sixteenth and seventeenth centuries—though he seems to date its beginning somewhat too early.

ordered bands of the Thirty Years' War."[153] Occasional atrocities, such as Louis XIV's demolition of the cities of the Palatinate, were relatively rare and always planned—not the excesses of marauding soldiery. Nor could the destruction of goods and life in these instances compare in magnitude with the damage to property and the killings of half a century before. Moreover, one European leader, William III, was relentless in his insistence on restraint. Stephen Baxter has described him as the originator of "humanitarian warfare," and there is no denying that his armies were able to make themselves tolerable to the inhabitants of the countrysides they occupied or traversed, not to mention the renown they gained for their discipline in battle. The Spaniards were apparently not far behind. The historian of the Netherlands sector during the War of the Spanish Succession makes the point explicitly: regulations to restrain atrocities took hold as pay and organization improved, and over the course of the seventeenth century "the behavior of soldiers" mellowed significantly. By 1700 the sacking of towns and villages, so common a hundred years before, was unknown.[154]

The results of this transformation emerge unambiguously from casualty statistics. At Nördlingen in 1634, of some 58,000 troops engaged in combat, close to 20,000 died—one-third. At Oudenarde over sixty years later 160,000 men killed fewer than 8,000 of their number—under one-twentieth. And the following year at Malpla-

153. Louis André, *Michel Le Tellier et Louvois* (Paris, 1942), p. 427. My translation. See, too, John U. Nef, *War and Human Progress* (Cambridge, Mass., 1950); G. N. Clark, *War and Society in the Seventeenth Century* (Cambridge, 1958), which dates the restraint at the very end of the century, a little later than most recent works; and Gordon B. Turner, *A History of Military Affairs in Western Society since the Eighteenth Century* (New York, 1953), which points to Westphalia as the turning-point. Another useful interpretation is Hans Speier, "Militarism in the Eighteenth Century," *Social Research*, III (1936), 304-36, a reference I owe to John Elliott. Speier emphasizes the work of Crucé in the 1620's, and the influence of the seventeenth-century ideal of *honnêteté*, as the sources of the restraint characteristic of warfare in the eighteenth century.

154. Stephen Baxter, "William III: The Professional Soldier in a Civilian Society," unpublished typescript. Hubert van Houtte, *Les Occupations étrangères en Belgique sous l'ancien régime* (Ghent & Paris, 1930), Vol. I, p. 55 and *passim*.

quet, notorious at the time as a peculiarly bloody encounter, less than 30,000 of the 200,000 involved died—about one-seventh.[155] Other casualty records are equally clear-cut, confirming a disparity far too great to be the result merely of improvements in reporting over a seventy-year period. At worst, therefore, the battles of the War of the Spanish Succession were considerably less than half as murderous as those of the Thirty Years' War. Despite vastly greater forces, they usually caused a fraction of the slaughter, even in a major engagement. Such figures speak for themselves, providing unequivocal evidence of the diminishing ferocity of war.

Could it be that the decline of religious fervor tempered aggressive instincts? Perhaps; but then one comes up against a chicken-and-egg problem, and my view is that the hatreds and conflicts grew so out of hand that they simply had to be stopped for that reason. It could be objected, too, that there are always critics of warfare. But what made these special was their original place within, not outside, the dominant groups of society. These were not anomalies like Castellio, whose pleas fell on deaf ears; nor were they a small party like the *politiques,* whose high-minded calls for peace provoked occasional sympathy but little change in behavior. They were, rather, pivotal figures like Locke; when *they* turned against war, one knew that a profound change had come over European society. And the best evidence, once again, comes from art.

Before we take a look at that evidence, however, the extreme tentativeness of the conclusions it suggests should be stressed. The next pages contrast with the rest of this essay in that they descend to a level of detail that thus far I have attempted to avoid. Their argument is still largely hypothetical, and is certainly not intended as a definitive statement or a one-dimensional solution to a most complex problem. Instead, they represent an attempt to establish

155. Wedgwood, *Thirty Years War,* pp. 361-67 (Nördlingen); the similar Lützen figures are in Roberts, *Gustavus Adolphus,* Vol. 2, pp. 763-72; for the later battles: G. M. Trevelyan, *England under Queen Anne: Ramillies and the Union with Scotland* (London, 1932), pp. 360-65 (Oudenarde), and *England under Queen Anne: The Peace and the Protestant Succession* (London, 1934), pp. 5-18 (Malplaquet), and pp. 18 ff. on the "bloody" image of Malplaquet; David Chandler, *Marlborough as Military Commander* (London, 1973), pp. 216, 221, and 252 ff. (Oudenarde and Malplaquet).

from primary sources a reasonable plausibility for the case I have put forward—namely, that the revulsion against the excesses of war was one of the fundamental reasons that stability returned in the mid-seventeenth century.

*   *   *

It was by no means uncommon for Renaissance and subsequent painters to make what were, in effect, political statements. Portraits had long served this purpose, even when they were not quite as blatant as Titian's Charlemagnesque *Charles V* (fig. 11) and herculean *Doge Gritti* or the Baroque's deified kings. Religious subjects, too, could have political overtones—for example, Botticelli's Savonarolan hail of fire on an unrepentant Florence that was the setting for his *Mystic Crucifixion*, and Tintoretto's depiction of *The Miracles of St. Mark*. But there were more direct ways to glorify the ruler or the state. Especially appropriate in this regard were military successes. Thus, starting with Uccello's stunning treatment of the battle of San Romano of 1432, almost every major victory had its heroic interpreters. If even minor engagements, by now totally forgotten, such as the battle of Cadore of 1508, could become subject matter for a master like Titian, despite the fact that, as Panofsky noted, "battle pieces . . . were not his forte," then really important victories like Lepanto inevitably unleashed a host of treatments, both allegorical (Veronese's as well as Titian's) and dramatically realistic (by Tintoretto, whose battles *were* his forte).[156]

The sixteenth and the early seventeenth century were particularly fruitful periods in the history of this genre. Swept up by the passions of the age, artists immortalized the aggressions of their rulers. Only one great figure resisted the tide: Peter Brueghel. Unique in the affection his canvases showed for the ordinary, cloddish peasants who populated Europe but were rarely painted, he was also unique in his outrage at the violence of war. His *Triumph*

156. Erwin Panofsky, *Problems in Titian Mostly Iconographic* (New York, 1969), p. 6; *ibid.*, Plates 83-88, indicate the tradition out of which the Rubens Decius Mus painting, illustrated below, fig. 14, emerged. Even Titian made a major contribution to that tradition.

(Foto Mas)

11. Titian *Charles V at Mühlberg* Prado Museum, Madrid

Charles V is here depicted at the scene of a great victory over the Protestants; such equestrian portraits, reminiscent of the chivalric knight, were frequent means of emphasizing the heroic (cf. fig. 17).

(Foto Mas)

12. Brueghel *The Triumph of Death* Prado Museum, Madrid

The entrance to hell, whose gate is raised, is in the right center of the painting; other crosses abound.

13. Brueghel *The Massacre of the Innocents* Kunsthistorisches Museum, Vienna

Alva is the figure in black in the middle of the detachment of cavalry in the upper center of the painting.

of Death (fig. 12) is not only a critique of social differentiation—a theme implicit in most treatments of this subject—but also a denunciation of the religious intolerance and persecution (represented by the omnipresent crosses, even on the gate to hell) that had arisen around him. And his *Census at Bethlehem*, showing his countrymen regimented during their hardest season by oppressive troops, is even more explicit. But his most unambiguous statement is the *Massacre of the Innocents* (fig. 13), set again in the Netherlands in winter, a scene of slaughter by Spaniards that is watched over by the Duke of Alva himself.[157]

No other artist followed Brueghel's lead until, sixty years later, the Thirty Years' War finally had the requisite effect. For now it was not a scornful outsider like Brueghel but the very pillars of the establishment who drew attention to the abyss that yawned immediately ahead. And what is especially revealing is that they had made their reputations, like so many of their predecessors, with glorifications of war. In that context the shift in commitments becomes all the more significant. For the surest sign of a radical transformation in consciousness or attitude, of revolutionary forces at work, is when men break with their own patterns. The tradition Brueghel came out of, and the kind of patronage he could expect, was entirely consistent with the denunciations that he painted. But the backgrounds of Rubens and Velázquez, and the buyers of their canvases, were of a completely different order. The last thing one would have expected from these pampered courtier-geniuses, viewing the world from above, not below, was an indication of the same concerns that had moved Brueghel. Yet that is precisely what appeared in the 1630's.

The case is strongest with the most appropriate painter of all, the epitome of the Baroque and its exaltations of power: Peter Paul Rubens. Not only did he idealize the militaristic kings and warriors of his day, such as Henry IV, Philip IV, Spinola, and Ferdinand of Austria (the latter specifically at the battle of Nördlingen), but he turned to antiquity for further elaboration of the theme of courage and prowess. When he was around forty he painted, together with

157. Stanley Ferber, "Peter Bruegel and the Duke of Alba," *Renaissance News*, XIX (1966), 205-19. See, too, Peter Thon, "Bruegel's *Triumph of Death* Reconsidered," *ibid.*, XXI (1968), 289-97.

van Dyck, a series of eight scenes from the life of Decius Mus, the consul of the fourth century B.C. who, together with Torquatus, had led the legions in the war with the Latins (one of the series, *Decius Mus Addressing the Legions,* is reproduced as fig. 14). According to legend, the night before the climactic battle both consuls had dreamed the same dream: that the general on one side, and the entire army on the other, were doomed to death. The two men had then agreed that whoever noticed his own wing beginning to waver the next day would go heedlessly forward so as to ensure his own and the enemy army's destruction. The events had unfolded as predicted, and Decius Mus had sacrificed himself for Rome (as did his son fifty years later). The choice of subject left no room for ambivalence, and indeed the treatment was fittingly magnificent. But this was 1617, the year before Bohemia dragged the Continent into war.

Some ten years later a different Rubens, weary and disillusioned by his failures as a diplomat, perceived the futility of the very qualities he had glorified in Decius Mus. By 1629 he was beginning to seek a way of leaving "the quicksands of politics," for their callousness and dishonesty had become, in the words of a recent biographer, "a source of incomprehension and distress."[158] He finally left diplomacy in 1635, but not before he had painted a poignant expression of his unease. The *Peace and War* of 1629 (fig. 15), presented to Charles I in 1630, when that monarch was making peace with both Spain and France, allows no mistake as to Rubens' preferences. War, and its storms and disturbances, are relegated to the background, and one of the two warriors looks over his shoulder in some surprise at the contented scene in the foreground. The Goddess of Peace herself, surrounded by symbols of the fecundity she brings, is a portrait of the wife of Rubens' close friend, Balthasar Gerbier, a fellow diplomat/artist. She and her entourage are bathed in light, in contrast to the darkness that surrounds war; and the light forms a kind of protective barrier for the group closest to the observer, consisting of the Gerbier children, for whose sake the entire scene has been fashioned.

But Rubens could be even more explicit. In 1638, three years

158. Christopher White, *Rubens and His World* (New York, 1968), pp. 95-96.

14. Rubens *Decius Mus Addressing the Legions* National Gallery of Art, Washington, D.C.

For other examples of such representations of generals exhorting their troops, see the reference in footnote 156. The painting has also been called *The Description of the Dream*.

after his retirement from diplomacy, he described his latest canvas, bluntly entitled *The Horrors of War* (fig. 16):

> The principal figure is Mars, who has left the open temple of Janus (which in time of peace, according to Roman custom, remained closed) and rushes forth with shield and blood-stained sword, threatening the people with great disaster. He pays little heed to Venus, his mistress, who, accompanied by her Amors and Cupids, strives with caresses and embraces to hold him. From the other side, Mars is dragged forward by the Fury Alekto, with a torch in her hand. Nearby are monsters personifying Pestilence and Famine, those inseparable partners of War. On the ground, turning her back, lies a woman with a broken lute, representing Harmony, which is incompatible with the discord of War. There is also a mother with a child in her arms, indicating that fecundity, procreation, and charity are thwarted by War, which corrupts and destroys everything. In addition, one sees an architect thrown on his back with his instruments in his hand, to show that that which in time of peace is constructed for the use and ornamentation of the City, is hurled to the ground by the force of arms and falls to ruin. I believe, if I remember rightly, that you will find on the ground under the feet of Mars a book as well as a drawing on paper, to imply that he treads underfoot all the arts and letters. There ought also to be a bundle of darts or arrows, with the band which held them together undone; these when bound form the symbol of Concord. Beside them is the caduceus and an olive-branch, attribute of Peace; these also are cast aside. That grief-stricken woman clothed in black, with torn veil, robbed of all her jewels and other ornaments, is the unfortunate Europe, who, for so many years now, has suffered plunder, outrage, and misery, which are so injurious to everyone that it is unnecessary to go into detail.[159]

This, from the narrator of the deeds of Decius Mus, was a recantation of awesome proportions, as was the "delightful escape . . .

159. R. S. Magurn, trans., *The Letters of Peter Paul Rubens* (Cambridge, Mass., 1955), pp. 408-9. Nef, *Cultural Foundations*, pp. 120-21, cites this letter as evidence of shifting attitudes toward war without, however, indicating the change it represented in Rubens' own career. Interestingly enough, it was only in the late 1630's that news stories, both in Germany and in a non-combatant country, England, began to stress atrocity and brutality as major themes of the war: see Schumacher, *Vox Populi*, chapter 6.

15. Rubens *Peace and War* National Gallery, London

During the same visit to London, Rubens also painted *The Blessings of Peace*, which again centers on the Gerbier children.

16. Rubens *The Horrors of War* Pitti Gallery, Florence

undisturbed by religious or political matters" that he created for Philip IV in the Torre de la Parada just outside Madrid.[160] In the remaining two years of his life, Rubens was often preoccupied with the series of landscapes which—yet again, in a notable break with his past—became one of his final testaments. And his very last undertaking was a set of four paintings that included two scenes from the story of the Romans and Sabines—a theme which joined anti-war sentiments with a classic instance of settlement and resolution.[161]

It is surely not irrelevant that the subject of the Sabine Women is attached particularly to this period in the history of painting. From Ludovico Carracci's treatment in the 1590's (not to mention Giovanni Bologna's sculpture of the 1580's) through Pietro da Cortona's in the 1620's and Poussin's in the 1630's, it held a peculiar fascination for the artists of the Baroque. These famous depictions certainly took advantage of the possibilities for dramatic action inherent in the subject, and that may have been its initial appeal. But one cannot escape the impression that its disappearance from favor after the 1630's (until revived by Tiepolo) symbolizes a major shift in the preoccupations of Europe's greatest painters. That Poussin should have chosen to paint it twice in the 1630's, in addition to two renderings of the *Massacre of the Innocents*, points to this decade as having affected others as it did Rubens.

Two prominent artists, in particular, can be added to the roster with some degree of plausibility. The first is Velázquez, almost the essence of the grandeur and arrogance of a Baroque Court. The favorite of Philip IV, he took his cue from Titian and showed not only the king and Olivares, but even the little prince Baltasar Carlos (fig. 17) in heroic poses on rearing horses. By depicting the first two in armor, he left no doubt as to his militaristic aims. However, a prominent historian of war, John Nef, has suggested that Velázquez' most famous painting of a military occasion, *The Surrender of Breda* (fig. 18), is in fact an anti-war picture. Considering the occasion, the insistent contrast between the Spanish and Dutch troops, and the immensity of the treatment, one has difficulty accepting such an interpretation. Yet there is no denying that the cen-

160. White, *Rubens*, p. 113.
161. I owe the idea of the double implication of the Sabine story to Erich Gruen.

ter of the interest is not an act of heroism, but a gesture of magnanimity; that the accent is not on the exultation of war but on the dispiritedness of the losers; and that Velázquez emphasizes the courteousness that is still possible in the midst of victory. One scholar has even suggested that the idea for the row of lances may have come from an etching in Callot's *Miseries of War*.[162]

For a less ambiguous statement we must turn to Velázquez' portrait of Mars (fig. 19), completed in the early 1640's. As the artist's most recent biographer, López-Rey, describes it, the figure is of "an unheroic god of war . . . a huge gawky figure, whose flabby torso, framed by broad shoulders and brawny arms and legs, sinks in a shade as his uncouth, dull and quite human features . . . shadow forth." Some commentators have tried to link the portrayal to an ancient *Mars* in the Villa Ludovisi or to Michelangelo's *Lorenzo de' Medici*, but López-Rey's dismissal of the resemblance seems well taken. What he does accept is the standard opinion that the painting is a satire of some kind, a joke at the expense of the ancients.[163] In that case, however, why specifically pick Mars? Given what was going on in Europe at the time, and especially what was happening to Spain, the choice of subject and treatment is surely a deliberate comment on war. This is not the usually vigorous, menacing God, splendid in his virility, but the tired warrior at the end of day. He has laid down his arms, and he contemplates, perhaps, the futility of his vocation. Rubens could express such distaste more openly, because he was a relatively independent man; for Velázquez, dependent on Court favor, a more oblique reference may have been necessary. Yet its impact is no less powerful than the more spectacular *Horrors of War*, and Velázquez, too, kept away from heroic subjects for the remainder of his life.

Our final evidence is the most straightforward. Jacques Callot, "the first specialist virtuoso etcher," in the description of Hyatt

162. Nef, *Cultural Foundations*, p. 121; Elizabeth de Gué Trapier, *Velázquez* (New York, 1948), pp. 223-24. It is possible, too, that Velázquez may have had chivalric conventions in mind, particularly in the slight bending of the knee of the Dutch commander, Justin of Nassau—a suggestion I owe to Orest Ranum.

163. José López-Rey, *Velázquez' Work and World* (Greenwich, Conn., 1968), p. 85. See, too, Trapier, *Velázquez*, pp. 261-63.

(Foto Mas)

17. Velázquez *Equestrian Portrait of Baltasar Carlos* Prado Museum, Madrid

The prince was either five or six years old when this portrait was painted (cf. fig. 11).

18. Velázquez *The Surrender of Breda* Prado Museum, Madrid

See below, fig. 21, for another dramatic use of lances by a contemporary of Velázquez.

19. Velázquez *Mars*
Prado Museum,
Madrid

(Foto Mas)

Mayor, began his career as a delightful decorative artist.[164] Both in Italy and in Lorraine, he was known for his Court scenes, his *capricci*, his interesting figure studies. He was known, too, for the ability to produce enormous plates, and in 1627 he was commissioned to produce a vast bird's eye view of the scene that Velázquez was to make famous, *The Siege of Breda* (fig. 20). Callot filled his panorama with sedate, almost idyllic vignettes of soldiers in camp, a representation of the conditions of warfare that he soon felt compelled to abandon, and that found no major echo in European art until the age of Watteau. For the late 1620's, however, the atmosphere still seemed right; his immense engraving (consisting of six dovetailing plates) was so well received that, like so many artists, he became a recorder of military victories. Accordingly, in 1631 he produced two more of his specialties: splendid and immense commemorations of Louis XIII's crushing of the Huguenots, the sieges of the Île de Ré and of La Rochelle. But then, two years later, and only two years before his premature death, he produced the masterpieces for which he is best remembered and which became widely admired at the time: the twenty-four etchings that comprise two series of *The Miseries of War*.

The title alone conveys the change of heart that came over this impeccable Court figure, closely allied as he was to the grandiose ambitions of his day. Some of the scenes seem to come straight out of Grimmelshausen, for despite the indignation the caption directs at the thieves shown in *The Hanging* (fig. 21), a closer look reveals their maimed bodies and their abandoned crutches. These are the victims of war as much as the perpetrators of its crimes. And the irony of the priest on the ladder, piously waving his cross at the corpses, cannot have been lost on those who saw the etching and were familiar with the religious passion that had justified the raising of armies in the first place. No less suggestive are two of Callot's last works: a *Martyrdom of St. Sebastian* (fig. 22), presented as a military execution, that looks like a scene out of the *Miseries* (fig. 23); and a *Temptation of St. Anthony* (fig. 24) which, unlike an earlier and more traditional version that he engraved in 1617, imposes an insistent military imagery on the devils who torment the

164. A. Hyatt Mayor, "Callot, Jacques," *Encyclopedia of World Art*, III (New York, 1960), p. 26.

20. Callot *The Siege of Breda* (detail) The Art Museum, Princeton University
This detail covers about a fifth of the full, immense vista.

Israel ex. Cum Privil. Reg.

A la fin ces Voleurs infames et perdus ,   Monstrent bien que le crime (horrible et noire engeance)   Et que ast le Destin des hommes vicieux
Comme fruits malheureux a cet arbre pendus   Est luy mesme instrument de honte et de vengeance,   Desprouuer tost ou tard la iustice des Cieux .   13

21. Callot *The Hanging* (from *The Miseries of War*)   The Art Museum, Princeton University

The lances in this etching have been proposed as a possible inspiration for the lances in the Velázquez *Surrender of Breda* (fig. 18). See note 162.

22. Callot *The Martyrdom of St. Sebastian* The Art Museum, Princeton University

23. Callot *The Execution* (from *The Miseries of War*) The Art Museum, Princeton University

4. Callot *The Temptation of St. Anthony* (detail)   The Art Museum, Princeton University

This detail covers about a third of the etching; St. Anthony, not shown, is to the right of this scene.

25. After Watteau *The Encampment* The Glasgow Art Gallery

The original painting has been lost; this copy is apparently by a near contemporary.

long-suffering hermit. The contrast, if we move forward some seventy-five years to Watteau's depictions of military life, could hardly be more vivid, or more revealing of the intensity of distress that had evoked such revulsion in the 1630's. Watteau's *Encampment* (fig. 25) resembles nothing so much as a pleasant, perhaps slightly melancholy, social gathering. The pain is gone; the "crisis" has passed; war has lost its horrors.

These tentative hypotheses obviously cannot sustain an entire theory about the reasons for the "resolution" of the succeeding generation. They are intended, rather, to point the way to a fuller exploration of the sense of accelerating disaster that appeared in Europe in the course of the Thirty Years' War. Many of the domestic upheavals of the 1640's and 1650's could be linked directly to the effects of that war, and it is not surprising that contemporary apprehension should have become widespread. As Trevor-Roper pointed out, Jeremiah Whittaker was by no means alone in believing that "these days are days of shaking . . . and this shaking is universal."[165] It was war, above all, that encouraged such beliefs—the mounting disruptions that led even the members of the Establishment, whose commitment was to the heroism and profits of fighting, to think of calm and relaxation as preferable to restlessness and ambition. And without this reversal among the upper classes, nothing else would have altered, because they were the linchpin of the *ancien régime*. Other considerations, such as their new alliances with central governments and their fear of social upheaval, certainly entered into their motivations, but the disillusionment with violence and confrontation was the first of the changes that eventually led Europeans to stop struggling with the consequences of the events of the early sixteenth century. New structures became acceptable, aggressions subsided, and aesthetic preferences softened: in sum, the "resolution" could occur, and the story that began with Columbus, Luther, and the "new monarchs" could come to an end.

165. "General Crisis," pp. 59-60.

XII

IMPLICATIONS FOR THE FUTURE

One of the instinctive predilections of the historian, as of the psy-
choanalyst, is for moments of high drama. We are drawn to periods
when things went wrong, and undervalue times when things went
right. It is the great upheaval, the explosion of new possibilities,
that arouses the most attention. There is thus an inevitability about
the choice of the decades around 1500, or at the end of the
eighteenth century, as the basic turning-points in European history,
for they witnessed rapid change, and change is the heart of our
subject. Yet what this essay claims is that periods of quieting down
may be just as important, just as full of watersheds, as periods of
rising up. We do not need to behave like Aristotelian physicists,
treating rest as a natural state, and seeking explanations only for
motion. The problem is that, like the psychoanalysts, we are
poorly equipped to study integration, stability, and the forces that
produce them. If my conclusions suggest anything, therefore, it
is the need to acquire that equipment. We have to understand what
it was that gave the late seventeenth century its sense of settlement,
how it can be differentiated from the preceding era, and especially
what caused the transformation. There is an excellent literature on
the means whereby wars end,[166] but very little on the calming effects that wars can have on succeeding generations, an influence
which could help explain the discontinuity of the mid-seventeenth
century.

Many areas of detailed research offer avenues through which

166. See particularly Paul Kecskemeti, *Strategic Surrender: The Politics of
Victory and Defeat* (New York, 1964); "How Wars End," a special
issue of *The Annals of The American Academy of Political and Social
Science*, 392 (1970); and F. C. Iklé, *Every War Must End* (New York,
1971).

these issues could be approached, but I can suggest here only those few which seem most clearly implicit in the preceding analysis. One obvious target might be the rhetoric of public declarations. Using the tools of linguistics and content analysis, historians might be able to discern shifts in the tenor of diplomatic correspondence, religious propaganda, discussions of grievances, or similar large, continuing, and fairly standardized bodies of material. If the number of inflammatory adjectives declined, or their intensity moderated, this would be excellent evidence of a change in perceptions, a calming of behavior.

Similar results might emerge from an investigation of the image and aims of warfare over the course of the seventeenth and the early eighteenth century. Can one detect a growing revulsion among thoughtful men, artists, and writers, or were pious platitudes the norm? Were defenders of war and advocates of heroism more or less vociferous at successive periods? Did they lose their audience when economics replaced religion as a major *casus belli?* And how extensive were the efforts to ritualize military affairs? Out of formalization arose the alleviation of violence, but all too little is known about such matters as the influence of military academies, the consequences of the transition from mercenaries to national armies, the development of new concepts of protection for belligerents, the wish to minimize losses—or how they can be linked to the decline in casualty figures. Equally unclear is the role played by political and economic motives—for instance, attempts to tighten governmental control and limit the devastation of prosperous territories—in sharpening discipline and blunting destructive forces after 1660. Moreover, much work still needs to be done on a number of straightforward topics, including strategic theory, battlefield tactics, and forms of training, all of which could have far-reaching implications for an understanding of changes in behavior throughout society.[167]

Another subject that would repay further investigation is the mechanism whereby the aristocracy throughout Europe was transformed from an autonomous pressure group, demonstrating its power through its ability to withstand a prince or a sovereign, into

167. Professor John Hale of the University of London is currently engaged in studies of some of these subjects.

a force for general control, closely linked with the central authority. It is a commonplace to speak of the "domestication" of the
nobility, but exactly how was that process accomplished? The re-
alignment is usually seen from the center, as if it were the product
simply of a series of policies promulgated by Louis XIV, Frederick
William, Leopold I, or William III. Yet so fundamental a reversal
can be accounted for only by a constellation of causes, including
the self-perception of the ruling class, improved communications,
economic pressures, political maturation, and a revolution in social
relations. Some of these topics have been probed by the literature on
the "seigneurial reaction," but it is a serious lacuna that the decades
around 1700 have attracted no works to compare with the studies of
Europe's aristocracies in the first half of the seventeenth century that
we owe to Stone and Bitton.[168]

A related problem is the reduced intensity and menace, and in
general the distinctive character, of popular upheavals after the
troubles of the mid-century died away. Scholarly attention has
fastened on periods of major turbulence, but the time of relative
quiescence, from the late seventeenth through the mid-eighteenth
century, is barely touched. The nature of violence tends to be
studied closely only when it is particularly persistent or subversive
—during the Reformation, during civil wars, or during endemic unrest like that of the 1640's. Its manifestations at less dramatic moments somehow seem less interesting, while the transitions from
one era to another have drawn almost no research. Tilly's article on
food riots is a notable exception;[169] clearly, far more work of this
kind will be needed before we can trace the fluctuations in the
nature and level of popular discontent. The necessity is all the
more pressing for times when disturbances were infrequent, because this is the subject that has been most neglected. Once a foundation of fact is established, though, it should be possible to embark
on the even more difficult task of explaining why grievances and/or
aggressiveness subside. That investigation would embrace many
varieties of destructive behavior—not merely lynchings of tax collectors and assaults on authority, but the killing of witches and the

168. Stone, *Crisis;* Bitton, *French Nobility*—see below, Bibliographic Ap-
    pendix, IV.
169. Tilly, "Food Riots"; cf. the literature she cites.

hunting of heretics. Some such effort to fill the notable gap between what we know about the causes of bellicosity and our understanding of its subsidence is long overdue.

Considerable progress has been made in elucidating one relevant issue, the changing goals of international relations, because this has long been the object of historical research. Nevertheless, the stages whereby religious and dynastic ambitions gradually gave way to the requirements of economics and national interest are still poorly defined. Although this is a well-trodden field, an imaginative approach to such matters as the growing influence of merchant communities on foreign policies, the collapse of ideological blocs, the reorientation of the aims and bases of alliances, and the bureaucratization of diplomatic procedures could be a means of answering much larger questions. In pursuing the consequences of the proliferation and increasing conventionality of diplomacy in the late seventeenth and the eighteenth century, for instance, one would be bound to cast light on the more general stabilization of European politics.

The most noticeable gap, however, is also the hardest to fill. And that is the paucity of general, comparative studies of the decades around 1700. Nothing like the "crisis" literature exists for the crucial years in the last third of the seventeenth century and the first third of the eighteenth, when a new political situation, new cultural forms, and new social relationships coalesced throughout Europe. Studies of this period remain as nation-bound, as uninformed by continent-wide themes, as the pre World War II literature on the seventeenth century described in the second section of this book. Whereas major advances have been made in reassessing the first two-thirds of the century, no such benefit has accrued to the last third, whose problems seem little altered from those which, more than a generation ago, absorbed Trevelyan, his contemporaries, and his predecessors.[170] The very revival of interest in the "crisis" period makes a broad rethinking of the subsequent era all the more imperative. This is particularly true if, as I have suggested, our perspective on the events of mid-century depends on our appreciation of their aftermath. Even without the framework of that particular

170. G. M. Trevelyan, *England under Queen Anne*, 3 vols. (London, 1930-34).

thesis, however, obvious benefits will accrue if scholars concentrate on the fifty years following the 1660's, and seek comprehensive reinterpretations of an age that is still viewed largely in terms of national histories.

To those pleas for further research I can add but one, possibly appealing, inducement: if times of subsidence can begin to merit as much investigation as times of eruption, maybe we will not have to resort to words like "crisis" to draw attention to a period. I am not sanguine enough to hope that "settlement" or "resolution," or even "struggle for stability," could serve such a purpose. After all, it would be futile to try to discard completely a conception that has been the source of so much illumination and whose wide dissemination guarantees that, historiographically, the seventeenth is likely to remain the century of "crisis" for a long time to come. Nevertheless, shifts of emphasis are probably essential if the controversies of the past twenty years are to avoid the danger of sterility. It must surely continue to be the task of specialists in the field, as it has been the aim of this essay, to promote the emergence of ever more coherent and all-embracing frameworks—frameworks with sufficient cogency, precision, and substance to give shape to the course of early modern history.

BIBLIOGRAPHIC APPENDIX

I. At Note 79: The chief works on political and historical thought are:

J. W. Allen, *A History of Political Thought in the Sixteenth Century* (London, 1928)

J. N. Figgis, *The Divine Right of Kings* (Cambridge, 1896)

Levi Fox, ed., *English Historical Scholarship in the Sixteenth and Seventeenth Centuries* (London, 1956)

J. H. Franklin, *Jean Bodin and the Sixteenth Century Revolution in the Methodology of Law and History* (New York, 1963)

F. S. Fussner, *The Historical Revolution: English Historical Writing and Thought 1580-1640* (London, 1962)

George Huppert, *The Idea of Perfect History: Historical Erudition and Historical Philosophy in Renaissance France* (Urbana, 1970)

Donald Kelley, *Foundations of Modern Historical Scholarship: Language, Law, and History in the French Renaissance* (New York, 1970)

Pierre Mesnard, *L'Essor de la philosophie politique au XVIᵉ siècle* (Paris, 1951)

J. H. M. Salmon, *The French Religious Wars in English Political Thought* (Oxford, 1959)

II. At Note 87: For a basic introduction to the issues of political stability and revolt in France, the following should be consulted (see, too, the works listed under the next heading):

William Beik, "Magistrates and Popular Uprisings in France before the Fronde: The Case of Toulouse," *Journal of Modern History*, 46 (1974), 585-608.

Leon Bernard, "French Society and Popular Uprisings under Louis XIV," *French Historical Studies*, III (1964), 454-74

Madeleine Foisil, *La Révolte des Nu-Pieds et les révoltes normandes de 1639* (Paris, 1970)

Pierre Goubert, *Cent Mille Provinciaux au XVIIᵉ siècle: Beauvais et le Beauvaisis de 1600 à 1730* (Paris, 1968), an abridgment of his massive, two-volume work, *Beauvais et le Beauvaisis de 1600 à 1730* (Paris, 1960)

Philip A. Knachel, *England and the Fronde* (Ithaca, 1967)

E. H. Kossmann, *La Fronde* (Leiden, 1954)

Emmanuel Le Roy Ladurie, *Les Paysans de Languedoc* (Paris, 1966)—English trans. by John Day (Urbana, 1974)

———, "Révoltes et contestations rurales en France de 1675 à 1788," *Annales*, XXIX (1974), 6-22

Guy Lemarchand, "Crises économiques et atmosphere sociale en milieu urbain sous Louis XIV," *Revue d'Histoire Moderne et Contemporaine*, 14 (1967), 244-65

Robert Mandrou, *Classes et luttes de classes en France au début de XVIIᵉ siècle* (Messina, 1965)

———, "Les Soulèvements populaires et la société française du XVIIᵉ siècle," *Annales*, XIV (1959), 756-65

———, "Vingt Ans après, ou une direction de recherches fecondes: les revoltes populaires en France au XVIIᵉ siècle," *Revue Historique*, CCXLII (1969), 29-40

A. L. Moote, *The Revolt of the Judges* (Princeton, 1971)

Roland Mousnier, *La Vénalité des offices sous Henri IV et Louis XIII* (Rouen, 1945)

———, ed., *Lettres et mémoires addressés au Chancelier Séguier, 1633-1649* (Paris, 1964)

———, "Recherches sur les soulèvements popularies en France avant la Fronde," *Revue d'Histoire Moderne et Contemporiane*, IV (1958), 81-113

Georges Pagès, *Naissance du grand siècle: La France de Henri IV à Louis XIV 1598-1661* (Paris, 1948)

Boris Porshnev, *Les Soulèvements populaires en France de 1623 à 1648* (Paris 1963), a French translation, with a new foreword, of a work first published in Russian in 1948

J. H. M. Salmon, "Venality of Office and Popular Sedition in Seventeenth-Century France," *Past & Present*, No. 37 (1967), 21-43

S. A. Westrich, *The Ormée of Bordeaux: A Revolution during the Fronde* (Baltimore, 1972)

John Wolf, *Louis XIV* (New York, 1968)

III. At Note 116: The following are some basic recent works on local history, plague, and demographic and economic trends (see, too, the works listed under the previous heading):

René Baehrel, *Une Croissance, la Basse-Provence rurale, fin du XVIᵉ siècle-1789* (Paris, 1961)

B. Bennassar, *Valladolid au siècle d'or* (Paris, 1967)

————, *Recherches sur les grandes épidemies dans le nord de l'Espagne à la fin du XVIe siècle* (Paris, 1969)

Fernand Braudel, F. Spooner, and Karl Helleiner, articles in *The Cambridge Economic History*, Vol. IV: *The Economy of Expanding Europe in the Sixteenth and Seventeenth Centuries* (Cambridge, 1967).

Pierre Chaunu, *La Civilisation de l'Europe classique* (Paris, 1966)

Carlo M. Cipolla, *Cristofano and the Plague: A Study in the History of Public Health in the Age of Galileo* (Berkeley, 1973), and the review by George Rosen in *Renaissance Quarterly*, XXVIII (1975), 83-86

Pierre Deyon, *Amiens, capitale provinciale, étude sur la société urbaine au XVIIe siècle* (Paris, 1967)

Christopher Friedrichs, *Nördlingen, 1580-1700: Society, Government, and the Impact of War* (Ph.D. dissertation, Princeton University, 1973)

E. Gautier and L. Henry, *La Population de Crulai* (Paris, 1958)

D. V. Glass and D. E. C. Eversley, eds., *Population in History* (London, 1965)

E. Helin, *La Démographie de Liège aux XVII et XVIII siècles* (Brussels, 1963)

Pierre Jeannin, *Merchants of the 16th Century*, trans. Paul Fittingoff (New York, 1972)

F. Mauro, *Le Portugal et l'Atlantique au XVIIe siècle, 1570-1670. Étude économique* (Paris, 1960)

Charles Mullett, *The Bubonic Plague and England: An Essay in the History of Preventive Medicine* (Lexington, Ky., 1956)

J. Nadal and E. Giralt, *La Population catalane de 1533 à 1717* (Paris, 1960)

B. E. Supple, *Commercial Crisis and Change in England, 1600-1642* (Cambridge, 1959)

H. van der Wee, *The Growth of the Antwerp Market and the European Economy* (The Hague, 1963)

E. A. Wrigley, *Population and History* (London, 1969)

IV. At note 123: Essential works in the literature on classes, mobility, agriculture, and rents, in addition to those cited under the previous heading and in note 118, are:

Davis Bitton, *The French Nobility in Crisis, 1560-1640* (Stanford, 1969)

Otto Brunner, *Adeliges Landleben und europäischer Geist. Leben und Werk Wolf Helmhards von Hohberg, 1612-1688* (Salzburg, 1949)

J. C. Davis, *The Decline of the Venetian Nobility as a Ruling Class* (Baltimore, 1962)

Alan Everitt, "Social Mobility in Early Modern England," *Past & Present*, No. 33 (1966), 56-73

Pierre Goubert, *The Ancien Régime: French Society 1600-1750*, trans. Steve Cox (New York, 1974)

Eric Kerridge, "The Movement of Rent, 1540-1640," *Economic History Review*, 2nd series, VI (1953), 16-34

Emmanuel Le Roy Ladurie and P. Couperie, "Le Mouvement des loyers parisiens de la fin de moyen-âge au XVIIIᵉ siècle," *Annales*, XXV (1970), 1002-23

D. Saalfeld, *Bauernwirtschaft und Gutsbetrieb in der vorindustriellen Zeit* (Stuttgart, 1960)

Lawrence Stone, *The Crisis of the Aristocracy 1558-1641* (Oxford, 1955)

————, "Social Mobility in England, 1500-1700," *Past & Present*, No. 33 (1966), 16-55

Joan Thirsk, ed., *The Agrarian History of England and Wales*, Vol. IV: *1500-1640* (Cambridge, 1967)

J. V. Vives, *An Economic History of Spain*, trans. F. M. López-Morillas (Princeton, 1969), 330-455

V. The following works of art, referred to in the text but not illustrated, are reproduced elsewhere, as indicated:

Giovanni Bologna, *The Rape of the Sabine:* John Shearman, *Mannerism* (Baltimore, 1967), Plate 44.

Botticelli, *The Mystic Crucifixion:* Gabriele Mandel, *The Complete Paintings of Botticelli* (New York, 1967), p. 109, Plate 150.

Brueghel, *The Census at Bethlehem:* F. Grossmann, *Bruegel: The Paintings, Complete Edition* (London, 1955), Plate 115.

Callot, *The Siege of the Île de Ré:* J. Lieure, *Jacques Callot*, VIII (Paris, 1927), Plate 654.

Callot, *The Siege of La Rochelle: ibid.*, Plate 655.

Ludovico Carracci, *The Rape of the Sabines:* Heinrich Bodmer, *Lodovico Carracci* (Burg b. Magdeburg, 1939), Plate 13.

Claude, *Moses and the Burning Bush:* Marcel Röthlisberger, *Claude Lorrain: The Paintings* (New Haven, 1961), II, Figure 262.

Pietro da Cortona, *The Rape of the Sabines: Encyclopedia of World Art*, XI, Plate 169.

Michelangelo, *Lorenzo de' Medici:* Adolfo Venturi, *Michelangelo*, trans. Joan Redfern (London and New York, 1928), Plate CXCIX.

Poussin, *Massacre of the Innocents* (two versions): Anthony Blunt, *Nicolas Poussin* (New York, 1967), Plates 14 and 46.

Poussin, *Rape of the Sabines* (two versions): *ibid.*, Plates 84 and 113.

Rubens, *The Apotheosis of Henry IV:* C. V. Wedgwood, *The World of Rubens 1577-1640* (Verona and Time-Life Books, 1973), p. 114, Plate 11.

Rubens, *The Cardinal-Infante Ferdinand of Austria at Nördlingen:* Carl Justi, *Velázquez y su siglo* (Madrid, 1953), Figure 61.

Rubens, *Landscape: The Castle of Steen:* Wedgwood, *Rubens*, pp. 182-83.

Rubens, *Massacre of the Innocents:* Giovanni Stepanow, *Rubens* (Milan, 1950), Plate 155.

Rubens, *Philip IV:* Wedgwood, *Rubens*, p. 20.

Rubens, *Rape of the Sabines:* Stepanow, *Rubens*, Plate 155.

Rubens, *Spinola:* R. M. Magurn, ed., *The Letters of Peter Paul Rubens* (Cambridge, Mass., 1955), opposite p. 208.

Tiepolo, *Rape of the Sabines:* Antonio Morassi, *A Complete Catalogue of the Paintings of G. B. Tiepolo* (London, 1962), Plate 300.

Tintoretto, *The Miracles of St. Mark: Encyclopedia of World Art*, XIV, Plates 80-83.

Titian, *The Battle of Cadore:* Erwin Panofsky, *Problems in Titian Mostly Iconographic* (New York, 1969), Plates 187-89.

Titian, *The Battle of Lepanto: ibid.*, Plate 80.

Titian, *Doge Gritti:* Hans Tietze, *Titian: Paintings and Drawings* (Vienna, 1937), Plate 98.

Uccello, *Battle of San Romano:* Paolo d'Ancona, *Paolo Uccello* (New York, 1960), Plates XLVI-LVI.

Velázquez, *Olivares:* José López-Rey, *Velázquez' Work and World* (Greenwich, Conn., 1968), Plate 77.

Velázquez, *Philip IV: ibid.*, Plate 75.

INDEX OF AUTHORS CITED

As a substitute for a full-scale bibliography, the following index lists the author of every book, article, and dissertation cited in the footnotes or the Bibliographic Appendix. Primary sources have not been indexed; only modern authors and editors are included. Translators have been omitted, as have writers whose works are not specified (their names, however, appear in the general Index). Also left out are those few books that give no indication of author or editor.

Since there are over three hundred listings, it seemed useful to divide the index into four parts, according to subject matter, so as to facilitate reference. When writers bridge two or more areas, present broad overviews, or center their work on the "crisis" thesis, they are placed in the first, general, category. The other three categories (political, social, and intellectual), while not totally distinct, are sufficiently definable to permit separate listings.

Only the first, complete citation of a title has been entered. In the case of a multi-volume work where the individual volumes as well as the entire set have been cited, only the first full reference is indexed.

The arabic numerals following the authors name give the number of the footnote in which the title appears. The italicized Roman numerals indicate sections of the Bibliographic Appendix.

1. General Histories and "Crisis" Studies

Aston, Trevor, 21

Chambers, Mortimer, 137
Clark, G. N., 7, 153
Clarke, Aidan, 29
Clough, Shepard B., 24
Crouzet, Maurice, 47

Elliott, J. H., 49, 53, 83, 84, 86

Gebhardt, Bruno, 92
Geyl, Peter, 91
Gilbert, Felix, 16
Graubard, S. R., 16
Green, V. H. H., 9

Halphen, Louis, 10
Hamilton, Charles D., 24
Hauser, Henri, 10
Hexter, J. H., 51, 81
Hill, Christopher, 23, 88
Hobsbawm, Eric, 3, 25
Holborn, Hajo, 85

Iklé, F. C., 166
Israel, J. I., 29

Kamen, Henry, 24, 86, 115
Kecskemeti, Paul, 166

Lavisse, Ernest, 84
Littlejohn, G. M., 49
Lublinskaya, A. D., 49
Lynch, John, 83, 84

Major, J. R., 24
Maland, David, 24, 126
Mandrou, Robert, 82, 128, *II*
Mariéjol, J. H., 84
Mauro, F., 49, *III*
Merriman, R. B., 7
Moote, A. Lloyd, 24, 53, *II*
Motley, J. L., 7
Mousnier, Roland, 47, 123, *II*

Nef, John U., 152, 153

2. Political, Diplomatic, and Military History

3. Social, Economic, and Demographic History

INDEX

Italicized numbers refer to the pages on which a painting by the artist is reproduced. The content of quotations has not been indexed.

Index

I wish to thank Susannah Rabb for her help in compiling this index.